PHOTOGRAPHY NOW

MARK HAWORTH-BOOTH

PHOTOGRAPHY NOW

DIRK NISHEN PUBLISHING

IN ASSOCIATION WITH **THE VICTORIA & ALBERT MUSEUM**

© Copyright Dirk Nishen Publishing 1989
Text: Crown copyright
Photographs: Crown copyright or as identified

This book was originally published to coincide with the
exhibition PHOTOGRAPHY NOW at the
Victoria & Albert Museum, South Kensington, London,
15 February to 30 April 1989

Designed and published by Dirk Nishen
London consultant: David Milbank Challis
Typesetting: Nagel Fototype, D-Berlin
Reproduction: O. R. T. Kirchner + Graser, D-Berlin
Printing: H. Heenemann, D-Berlin
Binding: Lüderitz & Bauer, D-Berlin

The publisher would like to thank Mark Haworth-Booth,
and all the other people who have assisted in the production.

ISBN 1 85378 012 X

Dirk Nishen Publishing
19 Doughty Street
London WC1N 2PT
Great Britain
01 242 0185

Front cover: William Wegman, Fay and Andrea (Folded),
1987 (see page 74/75)

This book is dedicated to the memory of Professor Peter Reyner Banham with gratitude and affection.

2
—
3

Frontispiece:
The Horses, No.102
Collection of Eugene and Barbara Schwartz, New York

CONTENTS

PREFACE

PHOTOGRAPHY NOW marks the 150th anniversary of the first public announcement of the invention of photography.

PHOTOGRAPHY NOW could not, of course, cover every interesting achievement in photography internationally from the last ten years (which is our definition of 'Now'). Instead, the approach is diagrammatic. We hope that the diagram suggests some, at least, of the important varieties of photographic achievement of the present and indicates avenues for further exploration by the new generations of the next decades.

PHOTOGRAPHY NOW shows exemplary – and thus illuminating – photographs drawn from the news, the photo-essay, personally chosen (or independent) assignments, fashion, advertising, photography as mixed-media installation, as portfolio or extended series, and, in particular, as book. From the first we decided to give a substantial place to publications – to celebrate the achievements in multiple production made possible by the positive/negative process invented by W. H. Fox Talbot and later by photo-mechanical printing (which he also pioneered). This is a period of exceptional, virtuoso, printing and we represent this in a section which could be called 'Places in Books'. We also show scholarly books, meticulous facsimiles and examples of that wide, popularising movement which is also a feature of photography in the 1980s. Other important categories feature the large themes. When Sir Henry Cole, the V & A's founding Director, acquired the first photographs for the Museum's collection in 1856, he bought examples of the nude, landscape, topography/architecture, still life and genre. PHOTOGRAPHY NOW looks at contemporary responses to these themes. However, PHOTOGRAPHY NOW also includes works which wittily elude convenient classification and we also added media which extend photographic language into the electronic era.

The exhibition on which this publication is based has been very generously supported by Agfa-Gevaert Ltd. Agfa was founded in 1867 and has become one of the best-known names in photography, supplying professionals, amateurs and the industry with the highest quality products. We are pleased to acknowledge our gratitude to the company and to its Managing Director, Mr Gustav Ahrens, for his help and his personal interest in the project.

The Museum is delighted to have the opportunity to work with Dirk Nishen Publishing, a company with a very fine reputation. We should like to thank Dirk Nishen and all his staff for their painstaking work against alarming deadlines. We are also very grateful to the artists, to their agents and – last but certainly not least – to the lenders who have very kindly allowed us to borrow works which greatly enhance PHOTOGRAPHY NOW.

Elizabeth Estevé-Coll

DIRECTOR
VICTORIA & ALBERT MUSEUM

PHOTOGRAPHY NOW

Photography has reached its 150th anniversary and arrived, simultaneously, at a period of unprecedented diversity, distinguished achievement and fundamental change. We can gain some sense of the distance photography has travelled and the imminent great changes, by looking back to one of the earliest surviving photographic images.

The invention of photography, in the form of the Daguerreotype, was first officially announced in Paris by Francois Arago on 7 January 1839. Arago (1786–1853), astronomer, physicist and politician, gained recognition for the inventors of the process and Government pensions for them – for Louis Jacques Mandé Daguerre (1787–1851) and Isidore Niépce (1805–68). The Paris announcement spurred the British inventor William Henry Fox Talbot (1800–77) to display his own invention, called 'Photogenic Drawing', at the Royal Institution in London on 25 January 1839. Arago fully disclosed the details of the Daguerreotype process at a joint session of the French Academies of the Sciences and the Fine Arts on 19 August 1839.

1 See Helmut Gernsheim, THE ORIGINS OF PHOTOGRAPHY (London, 1982), p.123, etc., for details of de St. Croix's demonstrations of the Daguerreotype in London.

2 Gavin Stamp, THE CHANGING METROPOLIS: EARLIEST PHOTOGRAPHY IN LONDON, 1839–1879, (London, 1984), p.9–12, etc.

Within weeks a M. de St. Croix travelled to London to demonstrate Daguerreotype.[1] He made Daguerreotypes in Regent Street and Trafalgar Square. Very fortunately, three of these pictures survived. The most extraordinary of the group was bought by the V & A in 1986 (after the Reviewing Committee on the Export of Works of Art had halted its departure from Britain to a collection in North America). Our plate shows – originally back to front, as is characteristic of the process, but corrected here – a vista of Whitehall from the corner of Trafalgar Square. To look at this Daguerreotype is to look at one of the first photographic pictures of a city.[2] THE TIMES described a street view by de St. Croix as 'resembling an exquisite mezzotint' – but it far surpasses the earlier process. It shines, on a silvered copper plate, which is solid to hold in the hand – but the image is evanescent, even when the plate is tilted to just the correct angle to the eye (like looking at a hologram today) and the street becomes magically present in all the exorbitant detail that the Daguerreotype possessed. This is one of the photographs which helped to form the earliest conceptions of the medium. It contains traces of people who are among the first to be photographed in city streets anywhere in the world. One is a cab-driver, whose hat, head and shoulders rise from the cab-stand at the right of the picture, between the globes of two gas lamps. Another, indeterminate – but male – figure sits at the foot of a street lamp, among bollards near Le Sueur's equestrian statue of Charles I. To the left of the sculptured pedestal of the statue is the afterimage of a third figure – silhouetted against the awning of a shop: the transparent hat, head and shoulders of another cab-driver. The names of the shops can be read – some with the naked eye, others only under magnification. Beginning on the left is a SWORD CUTLER. Next comes WILLIAMS. Then a GLOVER and HOSIER. To the right of the statue is the sign of a [B]OOK SELLER. A little further on is a shop bearing the royal coat of arms of a 'By Appointment' sign.

With a microscope the picture can be explored further still. The experience is unsettling, as if voyeuristic, and also uncanny, like a brief time travel, and absurdly pleasing. The startling lucidities are not unlike those shown in satellite photographs which reveal, from extravagantly long range in space, mundane details like the registration of a car parked somewhere in Kazakhstan. Presumably many of those who first examined this Daguerreotype were familiar with Whitehall and this row of shops and could read more with a naked eye. It is likely that this Daguerreotype was displayed by de

8 M. de St. Croix, Whitehall (from the corner of Trafalgar Square), 1839

3   LITERARY GAZETTE, 12 September 1839

4   Ibid.

11   M. de St. Croix, Whitehall (from the corner of Trafalgar Square), detail, 1839

St. Croix in the Argyll Rooms at 218 Regent Street or at the Royal Adelaide Gallery of Practical Science, West Strand – a few steps from the camera position at which the Daguerreotype plate was exposed. 'The minutest touch was recorded with magical fidelity,' said the LITERARY GAZETTE.[3] With a x 40 microscope, surface lines become visible – the lines caused by buffing the silvered copper surface to its state of high polish, in readiness for exposure – but the image does not break down into its constituent silver-mercury particles. The whole plate, with its glass window, feels substantial – it weighs over 260 grams. However, the surface could be accidentally wiped clean of its image, forever, as easily as tape. It looks, in fact, as if an incautious fingertip landed just above the words WILLIAMS and HOSIER – withdrawing hastily but too late.

A contemporary critic spoke of the 'low tone' of de St. Croix's Daguerreotypes. 'Many persons will be disappointed by the low tone of the image. Undoubtedly that is a great defect: it is impossible not to wish that, musically speaking, the piece could be played an octave higher. But the art is in its infancy; every scientific mind in Europe will be immediately directed towards the subject; and we predict that ere long improvements will be suggested in the process, which will leave nothing to be desired, either in that or in any other respect.'[4] Progress was rapid – but let us prefer to call it evolution, for Daguerreotypes achieved perfection of a kind (even though the process fell into disuse after less than 20 years).

Looking into the Whitehall Daguerreotype again with a microscope, the three blurs of grey on a white facade can be read as WRIGHT'S COFFEE AND CHOP HOUSE. You can see that the tall, first-floor windows have been thrown open. To the left, and two doors along to the right, are two structures which have survived from the time of this picture to the present – apart, that is from Inigo Jones's Banqueting House just visible on the same side of the street in a haze of sunlight. The bollards, still there, bear the cipher of William IV. Far into the picture are more shops with awnings. Extending from massive brackets are lamps to light the shop fronts. Inside these glass globes – part of what Henry James called 'the thick detail of London life' – you can see lettering put there by the shop owners, and just make out in one globe the word TEA. Someday someone interested in the way streets really looked at the opening of the Victorian era will read all these signs. The Daguerreotype will be able to repay almost endless attention. It was constructed in such a way that the information will not break down into stylization or gesture nor found to be synthetic – or false. The image has an integrity that is part of its physical make-up.

Fox Talbot continued to work on his own photographic process in 1839–40 and patented his positive-negative process in 1841. In THE PENCIL OF NATURE (1844–46) Talbot published his ideas and reflections on many aspects of the photographic medium. He delighted in the depth of its illusion. He also noted how photographs could contain details the photographer had not observed at the time that the lens was focused and the exposure was made. Only later, on the negative or the print, would the photographer notice for the first time, say, a sundial on a distant lawn. In the nature of the new medium, its transcriptions were unwittingly correct and – although exigencies like time might introduce abstraction – the evidence of a photograph was both mesmerisingly abundant and fundamentally verifiable. M. de St. Croix demonstrated these truths in London in the autumn of 1839.

Midtown Manhattan NEW YORK TIMES MAGAZINE 4 November 1984: straight shot (original in colour)

Midtown Manhattan NEW YORK TIMES MAGAZINE 4 November 1984: improved by computer (original in colour)

5   Jean Claude Lejeune/Black Star; Steve Proehl/Image Bank; J. P. Laffont/Sygma.

6   Lady Eastlake's essay is available in Beaumont Newhall's PHOTOGRAPHY: ESSAYS AND IMAGES, (New York, 1981); see Roland Barthes, CAMERA LUCIDA, (London 1982).

During the autumn of 1984 THE NEW YORK TIMES MAGAZINE demonstrated the new topographical photography of the 1980s. The Magazine presented two views of Midtown Manhattan. The first was a photograph by Gianfranco Gorgoni, a stock shot from Contact Press Images. The second was devised by the writer Fred Ritchin and NEW YORK TIMES MAGAZINE staff. They used the straight original as the starting point for perhaps the most elegant demonstration of photographic compositing by computer yet devised. It was published to illustrate Ritchin's article 'Photography's New Bag of Tricks' on 4 November 1984. We reproduce the demonstration here with thanks to Mr. Ritchin, the paper and the photographers involved.[5]

The amended view of Manhattan contains its eye-catching motifs: the Statue of Liberty has been conveniently relocated in a open space to the right of the UNO building, while to the left of UNO a scaled-down Eiffel Tower presides over East 42nd Street. The Chrysler Building has vanished – but in its place, magically, is San Francisco's Transamerica Pyramid (which is not quite in correct perspective). The Empire State Building has been moved a few blocks uptown. It has also gained a few floors. At the extreme right of the picture the top of the Citicorp Building has been spun through 180 degrees. There are ten alterations. The smaller ones are the most revealing, like the traffic jam created on E.42nd Street – done by repeating the existing cars in Gorgoni's photograph. The pier at the right is also disturbing – because it is an unobtrusive detail. Montage is hardly a new idea. It is as old as a hat pasted on a young man's head in a mid-Victorian family album. However, to fool with the trifles of which a cityscape is composed seems subversive indeed. It is, after all, the details which make photographs so compelling and authentic – from the 'very latch of the child's shoe' admired by Lady Eastlake in 1857 to the 'punctum' adumbrated by Roland Barthes in 1982.[6] Ritchin's demonstration had a serious purpose:

'The computer is at the heart of a revolution in image-making. It is now possible not only to make almost seamless composites of existing photographs and to alter images in such a way that the changes may not be detected, but – using mathematics instead of a camera – it is possible to create images that are nearly photographic in their realism. With the last technique, it might even be possible at some future date to "recreate" long-dead movie stars to appear in new movies.'

The pixels which make up an image on a digitized computer screen are like building blocks which can be coloured and combined in any way the operator's computer, competence and ingenuity allow. The same is true of video.

We are more or less aware of all this, even though it might come as a surprise to most viewers to discover how far news material is already being treated prior to transmission. Creative picture massage is a skill of the news departments as well as the drama studios. For example, if a public figure suffers a bereavement and no suitable image is available for transmission a stock photo may be amended to indicate plausible grief. Ritchin made another important point, however. Electronic cameras record light as a series of digital impulses on a magnetic disk. This eliminates the need for a darkroom, bringing an incredible advance in speed. However, 'the digital information can be easily altered, and there may be no permanent record as trustworthy as an original negative to determine what the image looked like when the film was first exposed'. The solid, silvered assurance of the Daguerreotype plate was dissolved long ago. The life of a photographic image today belongs in no one place, nor necessarily in any one form. The idea of a matrix, like the negative invented by Talbot, need no longer apply.

Perhaps, in the century of the movies, all this requires no great adjustment. We are all habituated to the synthetic magic of the cinema whereby, to quote from Robert Cumming's amusing meditation on the differences between still photography and film:

'An actor on location in Washington, D. C., might be filmed rounding the corner of Connecticut Avenue, striding up the walk, and on reaching the door, he gives the knob a turn, entering. It is April. Three thousand miles away in North Hollywood, in November, the man closes the door behind him and stands in the foyer taking off his hat. No one will notice the gap on the screen as one frame speeds past the projector bulb, across the splice, to the next frame. Adjusting to the disjointed ordering of time is like trying to adjust to the idea of massing all one's sleeping hours into the first couple of weeks of the month to have the remaining two weeks wide awake. If one were in the disjointed temporal mood, all one's bothersome driving to and from work could be compressed into several intense commuting marathons. Celluloid time is malleable, even reversible; the stability of real time meanders and comes under question the way many of our other unquestioned perceptions of solidity and certainty stumble in the confusion of deliberate sensory re-alignment'.[7]

7   'Studio Still Lifes' by Robert Cumming, APERTURE, (New York, 1985), No. 100, p.14

Still photography has the capacity to become as wilfully malleable as cinema. Luckily, however, we are very much used to cinema. News as fiction? That is not a particularly new idea either. The deconstruction of the old view of photography, as inexorably tied to 'reality', may bring with it a necessary sharpening of attention to the claims of all media representations.

Is this, the late 20th century, a time of revolution in the visual media? Or of accelerated change on lines with which we are familiar? No doubt we shall find out, but what seems to be true of this moment – 1989, when photography has reached the 150 year point – is that many different kinds of photographic image-making co-exist and are of equal validity. The fact that we can read all of these photographic versions of reality so easily and with such conviction is perhaps not the least astonishing feature of photography now.

As the Director explains in the preface, the exhibition was selected by looking at a number of separate modes of work, subject areas and photographic media. It is true that not every subject or application yielded work we thought matched the excellence we hoped for and had already found in some areas. We did not, perhaps by failure to look hard or widely enough, find any architectural photography that seemed to fit our purposes. We found instead a high general standard and – a very strong international body of work which is actually topographical, or environmental, rather than architectural. We had wished to include a section on the photographic book, as one of the characteristic vehicles of the medium of the 1980s. Thus, we chose books about places – or 'Places in Books'. This section includes with Richard Avedon's IN THE AMERICAN WEST, a work of extended portraiture which, nonetheless, is concerned with a place. We have stretched points, legitimately and logically we trust, in other areas of the structure. Fashion is represented by photographs by Bruce Weber which are not to do with selling clothes but with creating a style – which is, in other pictures, harnessed to fashion. It is the influence of Weber's style which has made him a phenomenon of the 1980s. Certainly, his impact owes much to the new advertising methods of his principal clients, Ralph Lauren and Calvin Klein – who, Michael Gross has written, 'spearheaded a new kind of fashion advertising, buying multiple pages in magazines, keeping their images consistent no matter what product was being advertised. Weber's photographs were given display that was unprecedented for anyone in fashion, particularly someone so young.'[8] This aspect of Weber's work needs to be elucidated at length – but the same is true of all the elements in this exhibition and book. The Museum will be investigating post-war fashion photography in depth in a show now being prepared by Martin Harrison and we hope to address other aspects of photography in greater depth on future occasions.

8   Michael Gross, 'Bruce Weber, Camera Chameleon', VANITY FAIR, June 1986.

The sheer abundance of the commercial use of Bruce Weber's imagery brings us to another feature of the selection here. One of the dramatic differences between the world as pictured by M. de St. Croix from Trafalgar Square in 1839 and the one in which PHOTOGRAPHY NOW takes place 150 years later is, precisely, the proliferation of photographically originated signs. The signs we can amuse ourselves by locating in a Daguerrotype under extreme magnification are, in the 1980s, all too abundantly clear to the naked eye. But they are not only to be seen on the street but within the mind's eye itself: the mental set has changed in the post-1960 years of unprecedented exposure to visual imagery. Perhaps the artists in this exhibition and book are united by only one thing other than that they have made use of some aspect of photographic technology: most of them are more likely than not to be familiar with the ideas of the French philosopher Jean Baudrillard. His work has proved to be perhaps the most widely influential cultural criticism of the 1980s – and it has direct bearing on photographic image-making and diffusion. 'The very definition of the real has become: "that of which it is possible to give an equivalent reproduction"' he wrote in SIMULATIONS (1983). 'The real is not only what can be reproduced, but that which is always already reproduced … the hyperreal, which is entirely in simulation'. To take a specific example, from the same book SIMULATIONS, it is not only possible to analyse Disneyland as a digest of the American way of life but such an ideological analysis conceals a further order of simulations: 'Disneyland is there to conceal the fact that it is the "real" country, all of "real" America, which IS Disneyland … Disneyland is presented as imaginary in order to make us believe that the rest is real, when in fact all of Los Angeles and the America surrounding it are no longer real, but of the order of the hyperreal and of simulation'[9]. So persuasive have Baudrillard's perceptions become that the 1988 US Presidential election was described by TIME magazine in his terms. Indeed, the magazine took the opportunity to address the whole post-1960 transformation:

9   Jean Baudrillard, SIMULATIONS, published by Semitext(e) Inc., New York, 1983, p.25.

'The elections of 1960 and 1988 are brackets enclosing a period of astonishing transformation – change that has placed the two campaigns in different eras. In 1960 the candidates for the first time debated on television, and politics began an almost metaphysical transformation: the external world was miraculously reconvened as powdered images upon America's internal screen. Electrons fetched out of the air poured the circus directly into the living room, into the bloodstream – just as they would inject Viet Nam into the centre of American consciousness.

This year represents something close to a dismantling of the American presidential campaign. The candidates perform simulations of encounters with the real world, but the exercise is principally a

10   Lance Morrow, , 'Of Myth and Memory: Dreaming of
      1960 in the New World', TIME, 24 October 1988, p.21.

11   C. Carr, 'On Quayle, Baudrillard, and Patti Hearst',
      THE VILLAGE VOICE, New York, 1 November 1988, p.38.

12   BRITISH PHOTOGRAPHY: TOWARDS A BIGGER PICTURE is
      the Fall 1988 issue of APERTURE, New York, and is also
      published by Aperture in book form.

series of television visuals, of staged events created for TV cameras. The issues have become as weightless as clouds of electrons, and the candidates mere actors in commercials.'[10]

New York's THE VILLAGE VOICE added the gloss that President Reagan 'was the first postmodern president, a "pure screen" and an "empty system of signs"'.[11] PHOTOGRAPHY NOW represents artists who function as artists, indeed, but also as cultural critics responsive to the new circumstances of the visual arts. (It is interesting to observe that perhaps the most influential art magazine in the West, ARTFORUM, New York, has in the later 1980s not only devoted special features and reviews to photography, but now runs regular columns on television, on news photography and on advertising). Thus, in this diagrammatic representation of photography, fashion is also shown in the curious mirror devised for it by Cindy Sherman, and advertising returns a regard shaped by the 'electronic scissors' – as he calls his camera – of Richard Prince. Advertising has reached, we believe, a quite remarkable development in the 1980s, and perhaps nowhere more than in the United Kingdom. (It will be clear that PHOTOGRAPHY NOW gives no special favouritism to work from Britain – but our belief that work here is at a very impressive pitch of creativity is echoed internationally, judging from the exhibitions and other attention from around the world, and much of the Museum's collection can be found in the Aperture publication BRITISH PHOTOGRAPHY: TOWARDS A BIGGER PICTURE, published in New York in November 1988).[12] We believe that British advertising is in a class of its own for inventiveness, elegance and sophistication. The campaign of Benson & Hedges has evolved remarkably over the past dozen years and has now reached a point at which the motifs chosen to dissemble the product are themselves classic symbols of dissembling – pretty fans for the summer months in 1988, attractive fishing lures for the autumn. The Government Health Warning beneath the images has now become merely a product identification sign – without the 'warning' we should not even begin to recognize what product was offered in the remarkable pictorial rebus above.

PHOTOGRAPHY NOW is planned then, as a diagram and a series of oppositions, or varieties. If diagram is the right word, we hope that it is like a set of arrows, or avenues, pointing outwards in some of the many directions an artist interested in photography might explore. The new directions to be taken may not be indicated by the diagram, or be unclassifiable by present terminology anyway – but they may have something in common with what is gathered here: ambition and invention, perseverance, independence, wit. It is because these qualities are so abundantly visible in photography today that the medium has some claim on our attention: photography still has much to tell us about the way the world looks and the experience of living in it.

Mark Haworth-Booth
CURATOR OF PHOTOGRAPHS
VICTORIA & ALBERT MUSEUM

CDP

Collett, Dickenson, Pearce & Partners
Spinners, 1988
Fans, 1988
Magazine advertisements and 48 sheet posters
Client: Benson & Hedges

'Potential clients still ask if we can do a Benson & Hedges campaign for them. When we sadly shake our heads, they may go and find some other agency that's willing to try. I don't think it would be immodest to say that it has done quite a bit to change the face of British advertising. It has certainly played its part in dramatically changing the fortunes of companies in the tobacco industry in this country. When we began working together, Gallaher was smaller than both Player's and Wills. Now it is larger than both of them put together'.

John Salmon, CDP

MIDDLE TAR As defined by H.M. Government
Warning: SMOKING CAN CAUSE FATAL DISEASES
Health Departments' Chief Medical Officers

The Benson & Hedges campaign from the London advertising agency Collett Dickenson Pearce (CDP) is one of the most admired in recent advertising history – and one of the longest running. CDP started working for Gallaher in 1962. The early campaigns seem to continue through to the very different style used today. The first task was to correct the public view that the product was more expensive than it actually was. Simple ads showed a picture of the pack, a half-crown and a two shilling piece. 'What can king-size smokers buy these days for two silver coins?' The answer was 'Pure gold at 4/6 for twenty'. The flat still life mode evolved into a series of elegantly constructed and photographed scenes which suggested pleasant smoking occasions and featured the pack (designed in the US in the late 1950s) as an upmarket object of value. 'Over the years, the voluntary regulations controlling cigarette advertising grew stricter', writes John Salmon, executive creative director of CDP. These regulations, set out in the British Code of Advertising Practice (the CAP Code) run to seven pages in the 1985 edition. An example is rule 2.10: 'Advertisements should not include copy or illustrations which are sexually titillating or which imply a link between smoking and sexual success.' By 1976 it was becoming difficult to ring changes on the "Pure Gold" theme and, Salmon adds, 'the public was becoming over-familiar with the campaign and it was being copied by rivals. An example of this was when we set up a shot on a Caribbean island with palm tree and sunset and 'Pure Gold'. When we finished, the photographer stayed on as another agency team moved in and shot an almost identical shot for a Player's brand – same tree, a sunrise not a sunset, a black pack not a gold one! Hastily we went to press first' (from CAMPAIGN, 16 September 1988). King-size had grown to represent 12% of the UK cigarette market. 'It had also become clear that the duty system would change to "end-product tax" which would greatly favour the king-size brands.' Salmon explains that 'Colletts and Gallaher agreed that to follow competition and cut price would show a short-term benefit in sales, but set up a long-term "imagery" problem. So we agreed to look for a new approach'.

Benson & Hedges began their new 'Surrealist' campaign in spring 1977 with a trio of 48 sheet billboard posters all displayed simultaneously. The familiar pack was shown, wildly improbably, propping up Stonehenge, as a canary, as a cat. It played these roles thanks to impeccable photographic skills, including montage and front-projection. The 'Fans' image which appeared on billboards and in magazines in summer 1988 changed the expected formula by dispensing with the pack altogether. Incomprehensible – at least at first glance – to those not familiar with the campaign, the image has much in common not only with British TV commercials but also with some branches of avant-garde photographic art in Britain which deliberately borrow cool and elliptical presentation techniques for other ends. The Benson & Hedges advertising budget for 1988 was £5 million.

18
—
19

Spinners, 1988
Magazine advertisement and 48 sheet poster
Photographer: De Zitter
Art Director: Nigel Rose

20 Fans, 1988
Magazine advertisement and 48 sheet poster
Photographer: Hugh Johnson
Art Director: Geoff Turner

ined by H.M.Government

S Health Departments'Chief Medical Officers

John Baldessari
The Fallen Easel, 1988
Lithograph with silkscreen on paper and metal
1880 x 2413 mm
Collection of the Victoria and Albert Museum

'... we, as Americans, understand our relationship to the world through various media. We think of any unknown situation in terms of something we've seen at the movies. That is the basis of our normal mass consciousness and how we see the world. John Baldessari is dealing with the archetypal consciousness of what media represent, using the material that affects daily life.'

Lawrence Weiner, 1986

'Metaphor is a figure of speech based on similarity, whereas metonymy is based on contiguity. In metaphor you substitute something "like" the thing you mean for the thing itself, whereas in metonymy you substitute some attribute or cause of effect of the thing for the thing itself,'
'I don't understand a word you're saying.'
'Well, take one of your moulds. The bottom bit is called the drag because it's dragged across the floor and the top bit is called the cope because it covers the bottom bit.'
'I told "you" that.'
'Yes, I know. What you didn't tell me was that "drag" is a metonymy and "cope" is a metaphor.'
Vic grunted. 'What difference does it make?'
'It's just a question of understanding how language works. I thought you were interested in how things work.'

David Lodge, NICE WORK, 1988

John Baldessari is one of the crucial figures in the re-direction of approaches to the visual arts in the past two decades. He was appointed to teach a course titled 'Post-studio Art' at the California Institute of Arts (Cal Arts) at Valencia, Los Angeles, in 1970. Although Cal Arts is now associated with a distinctive West Coast style, Baldessari was influential in bringing in East Coast and European artists – Joseph Kosuth, Robert Smithson, Lawrence Weiner, Daniel Buren, Hans Haacke, Sol LeWitt. He ritually destroyed his early paintings – a cremation at a mortuary, no less – in 1966. He asked himself 'Why do I have to cosmeticize everything by translating it into painting? Why can't I use straight information? Straight photography?' He became one of the first Conceptual artists and among the first to draw his imagery from television, movies, newspapers and advertising. 'The world constructed by the media seems to me a reasonable surrogate for "real life", whatever that is. I decided that aiming my camera at the TV set was just as reasonable as aiming it out the window' (ARTnews, Jan. 1986).

'The Fallen Easel' includes a pointed reference to the fall of easel-based art. Characteristically, this picture is not so much 'open-ended' as open all the way round. Baldessari's assemblages deal with moments of suspense derived from the movies. Glances shoot across the piece like gunshots. A revolver aims towards the spasm of a leaping fish. Discs of colour simultaneously identify and 'protect' (from identification) three sinister men in suits. A romantic comedy, or power play, is enacted above. The spectator is dropped into the picture, with its racing and contradictory trajectories, like Cary Grant into a Hitchcock plot. Baldessari parodies the strident demands of American media by setting them askew. The easel may have fallen but the picture somehow still holds up – just.

PRINCE   UNTITLED (COWBOYS)

Richard Prince
Untitled (Cowboys), 1986
Untitled (Cowboys), 1986
C-type colour prints, 686 x 1015 mm
By courtesy of Barbara Gladstone Gallery, New York

'I started to think of the camera as a pair of electronic scissors. The public images I would take didn't really need anything done to them. They didn't need to be silk-screened or painted on or collaged. The photograph that I presented had to resemble, as much as possible, the photograph that had initially attracted me. It was a matter of being as presumptuous as the original picture. I was interested in the camera as a technological device rather than as a mechanical one.'

Richard Prince, 1985

'Advertising images are presumptuous, as if they have their own ego. They're alien-looking, and at the same time so familiar they seem to have the possibility of being believed. They look like they have no history to them – like they showed up all at once.'

Richard Prince, 1987

Richard Prince initiated 'Rephotography' in 1977. He rephotographed four living room ensembles advertised by the same commercial manufacturer in magazines and made the photographs he had taken into a set of four works. These are reminiscent of Richard Hamilton's celebrated Pop Art collage 'Just what is it that makes today's homes so different so appealing?' (1956). Prince simply 'took' the photographs and they remain seamless. He photographed details from advertisements for watches and pens. A series of works compares the way cigarettes are displayed beside packets in magazine advertisements. 'I'm interested in what some of these images (that happen to be in the advertising sections of magazines) IMAGINE. I like the presumptuousness and the shame usually associated with these images. I like how unbelievable these images appear to be. How psychologically hopped-up a WATCH can look! I've never felt threatened by these images and certainly never felt compelled to buy what's represented in the advertisements. Sometimes, MOST OF THE TIME, what's represented is just wishful thinking. I'm interested in wishful thinking.'

25 Untitled (Cowboys), 1986

26 Untitled (Cowboys), 1986

Paul de Nooijer
Louis XV, 1987
Photographic decorations for Rotterdam Room, World
Trade Center, Rotterdam
Cibachrome colour prints on panels
Architect: Borek Sipek
Sponsored by Mobil Oil Bv
Temple d'Amour, 1977–80
Technical Highschool, Delft
Gelatin-silver prints on panels

Dutch photography is as varied as any, but there is a significant part of it devoted to play, theatricality and – in the case of Paul de Nooijer – both of these and public applications too. In 1977–80 he worked on a photographic mural for a Technical Highschool at Delft. The background illustrates three identical views of Le Notre's gardens in the grounds of Versailles, into which is inserted a Temple d'Amour. The columns of the temple continue into the real space of the school foyer.

An addition to Rotterdam's World Trade Center was built in 1986–87 and one part of it was set aside for a V. I. P. entertainment suite. The designer, Borek Sipek, commissioned Paul de Nooijer to make a series of photographic trompe l'œil decorations for the room. De Nooijer used photographs of Louis XV plaster mouldings in his house in Middelburg, lit with different coloured lights, as the basis of the design. These decorate the doors and ceiling – not continuously but as brief quotations. They embellish a pleasing but restricted space with colour, historical associations and humour.

De Nooijer's work here was commissioned by Borek Sipek, who left Czechoslovakia just after the Russian invasion of 1968 and is now based, with a studio of six designers, in Amsterdam. 'Of the new designers who have emerged at the Milan fairs over the past few years, Borek Sipek has one of the most distinctive and personal visions' – Deyan Sudjic, BLUEPRINT, November 1988, p. 44.

The same plasterwork motif, lit with orange, purple and green lights, was used by de Nooijer for a wall decoration in the main entrance of the Social Welfare office in Middelburg in 1988.

In a recent essay on de Nooijer, Hripsimé Visser describes his enthusiasm for the baroque; a de Nooijer mural for a school in Nieuwegein is called D'UNE MANIÈRE BAROQUE (1985). She goes on to point out that 'Nothing was more alien to the baroque than a puritanical attitude towards technique and material. So long as the intended effect was achieved all means were justified: architecture, ornament, sculpture, painting, all the arts were to serve the optical illusion. In fact the CAMERA even played an essential role in the baroque. Perspectival TRICKS were impossible without a thorough knowledge and application of the camera obscura ...' Possibly photography may have a new life as trompe l'œil.

28 Louis XV, 1987
© LJAD, Creyghton

29 Temple d'Amour, 1977–80

Martin Cleaver
HMS Antelope exploding, San Carlos Bay, East Falkland
1982
Gelatin-silver print 406 x 508 mm
Collection of the Victoria & Albert Museum

This is an example of a hard news photograph that – by recording one instant – seems to represent a whole episode, the Falklands War, and in turn a whole era of national history. It also illustrates the way in which many news photographs are taken, some of the constraints news photographers work under, and the virtues of the still against a moving image. The story has been told by Kate Salway:

'Martin Cleaver was watching HMS ANTELOPE in "Bomb Alley", San Carlos Bay, East Falkland on May 25th, 1982, from the Royal Fleet Auxiliary STROMNESS about half a mile away. He knew that a bomb disposal man had failed to defuse safely the Argentine bomb lodged in the frigate's engine room, which had exploded, killing him, and that had started a fire on board.

From up on the superstructure of STROMNESS he saw all the men on ANTELOPE being mustered on the flight deck and being taken off. He realised that they couldn't put the fire out and that something was going to happen. He thought, "If that's going up it's going to be big". That "something" happened three hours later, when Martin, cold and tired but still with his Nikon FM2 and 300 mm lens around his neck, suddenly saw that the ship was about to explode. Instinctively, his camera went up – click – and it was all over. He'd shot hand-held at a fifteenth of a second at f4.5.'

He processed his film and hid it. On a previous occasion, when he was flying over the stricken HMS SHEFFIELD, nine-tenths of his negatives had been removed. However, news of the explosion had been broadcast and after 24 hours Cleaver's picture was cleared by the Ministry of Defence and transmitted to London. It was not only widely used at once but became the "identification photograph" of the war. The explosion had been filmed by a BBC TV cameraman, Bernard Hesketh, but was over too quickly to have any impact.

Sebastião Salgado
The Serra Pelada Goldmine, Brazil, 1987
Gelatin silver prints on 406 x 508 mm paper
Collection of the Victoria & Albert Museum

'It is a staggering scene, seeming to belong in a time in which slaves built monumental works for pharaohs and kings. The ancient, frenzied dream of gold has drawn 400,000 people across the wilderness of Brazil. Digging in the Amazon forests, diving into rivers and gnawing at mountainsides, they move with the rainy season and rumours of new sites. Serra Pelada, in the northern state of Para, is the largest and richest of these improvised mines. Since a peasant found the first nuggets there in 1980, a mountain has been reduced to a hollow 600 feet deep and half a mile wide.'

Marlise Simons, THE NEW YORK TIMES MAGAZINE,
7 June 1987

Salgado photographed at the mine for three weeks. He had decided to undertake an epic enterprise – to photograph 'The Archaeology of the Industrial Era: Manual Labour at the Dawn of the 21st Century'. He had chosen 40 manual occupations. This was the first. From a take of about 100 useable pictures, his agency – Magnum Photos with offices in Paris, New York, London and Hamburg – selected about 30 subjects for distribution to the magazine press world-wide. Salgado was not the first to photograph this extraordinary spectacle. It also appears in the feature film WHERE THE RIVER RUNS BLACK. However, it was Salgado's pictures which caught the imagination of picture editors. They were published around the world during 1987, beginning in MANCHETE, (Brazil) 16 May ('Serra Pelado – A Torre de Babel desce ao inferno'), followed by THE SUNDAY TIMES MAGAZINE, London, on 24 May ('In the Hellhole') and then in THE NEW YORK TIMES MAGAZINE, 7 June ('An Epic Struggle for Gold').

Salgado's photo-essay was a major commercial success and reached an audience measured in many tens of millions. He is continuing his five year project on manual labour, which will be shown periodically in special issues of the newspaper LIBERATION, Paris, and finally in a large-scale exhibition and publication.

Serra Pelada ('Bald Mountain') is in the south eastern Amazon basin. Gold was found by chance – according to legend, a cowherd picked a nugget from a stream – in 1980. A goldrush began at once. 'At the time, settlers were already cutting and burning great stretches of jungle for many miles around for agriculture, forced into the region by poverty in their own territories. Only a few hours' drive by dirt highway from Serra Pelada, the government was pouring investment into the construction of an immense mining project called Carajas, a mountain range of solid iron. The gold discovery brought settlers dashing from their black and smouldering jungle clearings to stake claims on the ore-bearing land, and construction workers abandoned Carajas to join the rush' (from Robert Tyrer's report in THE SUNDAY TIMES MAGAZINE, 24 May 1987). The mountain has become a pit. At times up to 150,000 'garimpeiros', gold-prospectors, worked the 6 sq m plots, 'barrancos', into which the site was divided. There were 6,400 claims, or concessions, whose owners employed the miners. 42 tons of gold had been extracted by 1987, with one nugget weighing 63.39 kilos. Soil was scraped away and carried up ladders in bags, weighing 30–60 kilos, to be dumped at the edge of the crater. The mine has since – with violent and fatal opposition – been placed under government control. Landslides had claimed lives earlier; chemicals used in leaching gold from earth threatened the health of the 'garimpeiros', while mercury contaminated the rivers.

Salgado's photo-essay opens a window onto a world that seems authentically antique – as far off as when the Pyramids were being built – but it presumably touched a nerve with editors because it is also a parable of greed with global relevance.

Frank Gohlke
Mount St. Helens, 1981–82
Gelatin silver prints, 406 x 508 and 508 x 600 mm
Collection of the Victoria & Albert Museum

'Some facts: On May 18, 1980, Mt. St. Helens in the Cascade Range of southwestern Washington state erupted explosively, two months after the first signs that a 123-year period of dormancy was ending. An earthquake caused the weakened north face of the mountain to avalanche into the Tourle River valley, instantaneously releasing the pressure on the upwelling magma below. The result was a lateral blast of incredible force that devastated 230 square miles of commercial timberland, recreational forest and wilderness. Trees representing one billion board feet of timber were killed where they stood, flattened, pulverized and blown away. Valleys were filled with debris, rivers were rerouted, old lakes were reshaped and new lakes created. Where before there had been a gleaming, symmetrical cone 9700 feet high, there was now a gaping horseshoe-shaped crater whose rim was 3000 feet lower than the old summit. Perhaps two million animals of all species were killed, including 65 human beings. During the seven hours of the May 18 eruption the release of energy was estimated to equal one Hiroshima-sized bomb per second.'

Frank Gohlke

The earthquake and eruption in 1980 were epic in the strict sense of being of national and supra-national proportions. Ash from Mt. St. Helens reached an altitude of 6000 metres in 10 minutes. It caused hazy skies and red sunsets around the globe. The explosion rivalled Vesuvius, Pelee and others of the historical era.

Hundreds of amateurs and professionals photographed the event. A news photographer was killed.

Frank Gohlke photographed the aftermath of the eruption, returning each summer for four years. He worked from helicopters and on the ground. Gohlke tells a more subtle story than made the early headlines. His photographs seem to do justice to the epic immensity of the subject, but also its symbolic implications. His photographs are complex and sometimes ironic. He shows the way 'clearcutting' by the US Forestry Service is registered as bald scars on the mountain ranges – hard to distinguish at once from the destruction caused by natural forces. Ash on snow, snow on ash, make the forms of landscape illegible. Man's place in these photographs is indicated, apart from the miles of clearcut ground, by tiny trucks and a speck-sized helicopter touched down in a clearing: Man seems like an adventurer who occurs somewhat late in geophysical history and his influence on the earth's surface seems incommensurate with either his scale or his significance. Gohlke has written thoughfully about the way in which photographs can appear to embrace features of the past, the present and the future: 'Projecting oneself into the future so that one can view the present with more apparent dispassion, and projecting an image of the past onto the future in order to take the measure of the present are different strategies. But both are attempts to make the present transparent to a more inclusive and fluid sense of time and consequence' (APERTURE, No.98). His Mt. St. Helens photographs exemplify this transparency.

Lee Friedlander
Factory Valleys and Cray
'Factory Valleys', 1979–80
'Cray at Chippewa Falls', 1986
All gelatin-silver prints on 279 x 355 mm paper
By courtesy of Zabriskie Gallery, New York

'Let me tell you one thing, what they say has a great deal to do with what they do, and what they do they do do, as what they were was part of what they did, as by the time, this time, they are what they are.
How do they know what they are. They know it by looking at what they do. This is why the United States of America is important.'

SCENERY AND GEORGE WASHINGTON or A HISTORY OF THE UNITED STATES OF AMERICA by Gertrude Stein (quoted from the epigraph to FACTORY VALLEYS)

Lee Friedlander exhibited with Garry Winogrand and Diane Arbus in a landmark show called 'New Documents' organized by the Department of Photography at The Museum of Modern Art, New York, in 1966 (which toured the US 1967–75). By the late 1970s he was established as perhaps the wittiest and most penetrating photographer of American cities and their paraphernalia of competing sign-languages. He was not regarded as a photographer of, for example, American industry. In 1979 John Coplans, then director of the Akron Art Museum, invited Lee Friedlander to photograph the northern industrial belt of the United States. Friedlander eventually focused the project on Ohio and Pennsylvania and photographed for about 13 weeks in the different seasons during the course of a year. The results were published in the book FACTORY VALLEYS in 1982. No photographer has better described manual labour in the heavy industries, or the settlements in which these industries are sited.

Cray Research, Inc. build supercomputers in Chippewa Falls, in farm country in Minnesota. They invited Friedlander to photograph their factory and the locality in 1986. CRAY AT CHIPPEWA FALLS was published by the company to mark its fifteenth anniversary in 1987. Friedlander used many of the formal devices he developed during the earlier series but also conveyed the different working environment of a new, light industry. What he observed in both series rings true of many kinds of work, in which materials impose on the operator and attention fixes a person to a task. The Cray project is a model of effective industrial initiative in the visual arts. The book shows not only how people work but how small American towns work. That is another subject Friedlander has made his own – but his example could be productively followed anywhere.

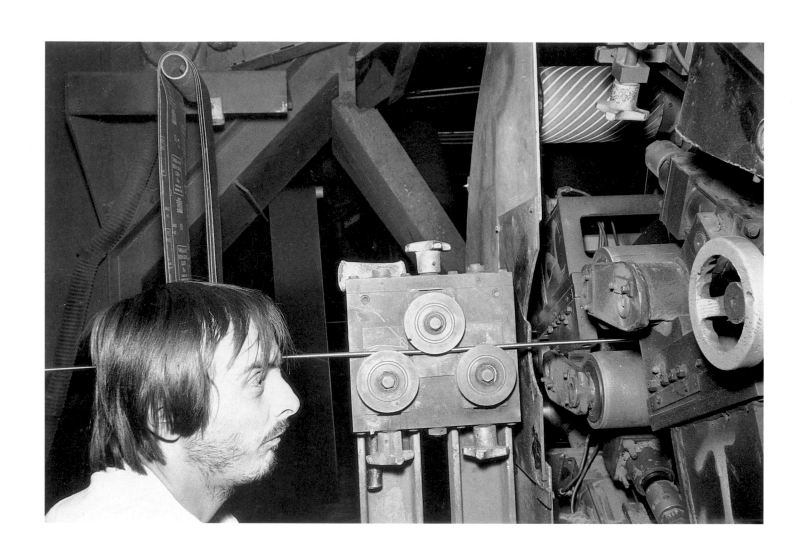

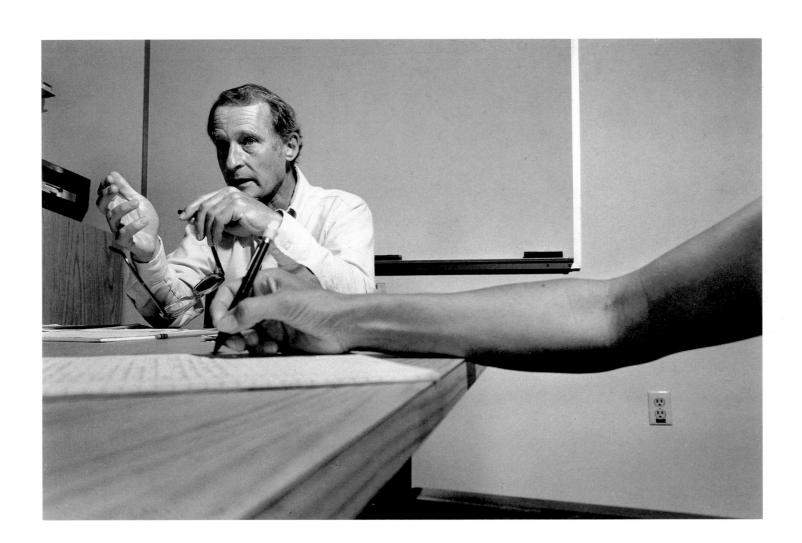

NIXON   THE BROWN SISTERS

Nicholas Nixon
The Brown Sisters 1975, 1978, 1980, 1984, 1987
Gelatin-silver prints, each 203 x 254 mm
By courtesy of Zabriskie Gallery, New York

'One might expect that the systematic structure of the series – the fixed sibling relation of the four women in a row, the unvarying interval of time – might give it a quasi-scientific aspect, as if it might be used as reliable evidence. In fact the series presents a fluid image of time, complex with eddies and pools, swells and calms. Each portrait, stable in isolation, is qualified by a rich store of resemblances and differences, which cannot be reconciled to a single linear narrative. Age, identity, family relation are not pictured as fixed qualities but as pliable threads within a fertile and provisional view of experience.'

Peter Galassi

'I love to photograph people: their skin, their stances, the space around them. The picture is the point: the clearer and more beautiful the better.'

Nicholas Nixon

Nixon's photographic materials are as traditional as can be and his idea was a very simple one. Using an 8 x 10 inch view camera and black and white film, from which he makes contact prints, he has photographed his wife and her three sisters annually since 1975. The result is already among the masterpieces of portraiture in the photographic medium. The series also shows with absolute clarity what the medium can do (that other media cannot). Photography can measure time by stopping it. However, it is curious to find, looking at this series of photographs, that biography appears to progress in a manner which is not linear but cyclical. Experience seems to evolve from youth in a way not measured by the calendar: more like a river than a canal – which is what we knew but never saw so clearly as in these photographs. The series prompts the question: How can we settle for a portraiture less complex than this? The series is an object lesson in, among many other qualities, the differences of gaze. Most viewers who ponder the matter can decide – from looking at the eyes – which of the four sisters is married to the photographer.

In a recent essay Peter Galassi describes the framework of the series: 'With the second picture, in 1976, the five participants settled upon two constants: a single picture a year (no matter how many negatives Nixon exposed or how good the alternatives) and an unvarying line-up (from left to right: Heather, Mimi, Bebe, Laurie). A third, unstated constant was that each of the four women would look at the camera, and that each should be not just physically but psychologically present ...

In 1975 the Brown sisters ranged in age from fifteen to twenty-five. In other words, the series begins at the threshold of adulthood, when expectation has not yet been revised by experience. It begins at a beginning and thus promises the whole of a life.'

Nancy Burson
(with David Kramlich and Richard Carling)
Warhead I (Reagan 55 %, Brezhnev 45 %), 1982 (Copyright 1982)
Big Brother (Stalin, Mussolini, Mao, Hitler and Khomeini) 1983 (Copyright 1983)
Mankind, 1983–85 (Copyright 1983–85)
Gelatin-silver prints, 406 x 508 mm
By courtesy of the Holly Solomon Gallery, New York

'... some wizard is lurking undiscovered out in the world, waiting to take the right faces and meld them just the right way into faces that never did exist except in the hypothetical. Likely as not, those faces will eventually be animated on film or video. Hypothetical people, who never existed in the flesh but are composites of different citizens' features and voices, will dance across our screens.'

Art Kleiner, Aperture 106, 1987

'Burson's work reminds us that we are all composites, fusions of other lives, fusions of many people.'

William A. Ewing and Jeanne A. McDermott, 1986

These composite photographs were made by the artist Nancy Burson with the aid of two creative computer scientists, David Kramlich and Richard Carling. Working with a video camera capable of converting an image into digital form, a computer and a specially designed software programme, the trio were able to create photographically convincing composite portraits. The video camera scans photographs (or, of course, a real person) and encodes the image into pixels – picture elements or numerical values that correspond to the lightness or darkness of the image. The face on the computer screen is seen through a grid which divides into 512 horizontal and 480 vertical squares. The pixels can be enlarged until a few of them fill the screen and detailed manipulation can be done. A key feature of the procedure is the use of a 'warping grid', which allows one image to be stretched so that its proportions match those of another. The creation of a convincing composite requires interpretive (subjective) decisions. Once the composite on screen has reached a satisfactory state it is photographed with a standard 35 mm camera. The proportions of the mix in the Reagan/Brezhnev head are based on the number of nuclear warheads in each leader's arsenal. The 'Big Brother' image was made for use as a background blow-up in a Walter Cronkite CBS television film on Orwell's 1984. Burson has also made images of missing children, aged by computer, for their families and for the FBI.

61   Warhead I, 1982

62   Mankind, 1983–85

63   Big Brother, 1983

Cindy Sherman
Untitled, 1983
C-type colour prints
Untitled (No. 123), 1983
911 x 611 mm
By courtesy of Pamela and James Heller, New York City,
New York, USA
Untitled (No. 118), 1983
878 x 592 mm
By courtesy of Mr and Mrs Robert Kaye, West Long
Branch, New Jersey, USA
Untitled (No. 119), 1983
446 x 916 mm
By courtesy of Ellen Kern, New York City, New York, USA

'Working against fashion she has made her work less specifically feminine, her characters less compliant. Abusing her face with unflattering makeup and strange expressions has given her more range as an actress. And in being so extreme, so peculiarly off, these images don't rely on a cumulative reading for their falseness to come across... Sherman's thinking on these matters is, as usual, hard to read – sometimes she seems like the best naive artist around. She just keeps throwing these images together and they just keep setting off, inevitably, a certain number of possible meanings in the viewer's mind. Her ability to keep on doing this is admirable and a bit amazing – her career threatens to become an endurance test that everybody is watching.'

Roberta Smith, THE VILLAGE VOICE, 29 November 1983

'It [Cindy Sherman's retrospective at the Whitney Museum of American Art, 1987] is a very unsettling show. When I left, I saw Sherman, like a figural after-effect, absolutely everywhere – in the jeans ads on the back of buses, on the television screens in video shops, on the front pages of tabloids, in the ads of The New Yorker... and in the mannequins in Madison Avenue storefronts.'

Arthur C. Danto, THE NATION, 15–22 August 1987

Cindy Sherman's art is one of the defining forces of the 1980s. Her series of UNTITLED FILM STILLS (pictures of herself in imaginary movie scenarios) tapped a reservoir of imagery of unexpected power and subtlety. She followed the film stills with a series which took the convention of the centrefold pin-up and twisted it with a gauche naturalness – creating an awkward, sharp, counter-attack on voyeurism. In 1983 she was invited by the Dianne B. clothes shops in New York City to make fashion advertisements featuring herself and clothes by top designers – Issey Miyake (seen in UNTITLED, NO.118) and Dorothée Bis (seen in UNTITLED, NOS.119, 123), and others. Sherman agreed, on condition that she could also use the clothes in her personal work. Advertisements appeared in INTERVIEW magazine in 1983, in grainy black and white on newsprint. The magazine BOMB, no. 5, 1983, includes both a full-page black and white advertisement in which Sherman models Issey Miyake clothes, somewhat in the guise of a wrongly strung marionette, and – elsewhere in the magazine – a personal picture in which Sherman appears in the same clothes as an exotic, diva-like force. Her art is most succesful when she takes on archetypal roles and makes her audience aware, simultaneously, of how immediately recognizable, widely shared and transparently obvious these roles are. She shows how the individual (artist) can oppose corporate image-making by using what lies around at home, plus the traditional methods of parody, satire and humour: of taking an image 'too far' or nowhere near far enough. She used the fashion commission to extend the range of her mythic roles – a nightclub chanteuse, a Brunhilde, plus more familiar cinematic figures, such as the desert rose, and an overripe, vampish bather, plus a giantess, who gazes heavily at the camera from a beautiful Issey Miyake creation which 'sets off' the colour of the bandage on her finger. The series is a variation of Hans Christian Andersen's fable of the Emperor – and it is more rather than less pointed because here the clothes are fabulous.

70 Untitled (No. 123), 1983

71 Untitled (No. 118), 1983

72
—
73 Untitled (No. 119), 1983

William Wegman
Fay and Andrea (Folded), 1987
Polacolor II photograph, 610 x 508 mm
Lent by Mrs Robert Greenhill, Greenwich, Conn.
Fay/Ruscha, 1987
Polacolor II photographs (diptych), each 610 x 508 mm
Lent by The Museum of Modern Art, New York
Dressed for Ball, 1988
Polacolor II photograph, 610 x 508 mm
By courtesy of Pace/MacGill Gallery, New York

'Wegman says he "had a revelation in the 60s – don't
work over your own head".'

Amy Hempel

'The dog's silvery-tan coat glows with different tints
against pink, beige, or brown. Fay Ray is an eloquent
heroine for a stylish era: good bones and colouring,
the perfect figure for clothes, and eager for exposure.
What a bitch!'

Vicki Goldberg

William Wegman usually appears in books on the art of the last two decades in his role as a pioneer Conceptual artist – and in particular as author of a piece called 'Family Combinations' (1972). This work used double-printing (overlaying two negatives and printing one image from them) to combine portrait photographs of Wegman, his father and his mother. The resulting six photographs, arranged side by side in two rows, have been well described by Andy Grundberg as 'at once an act of genetic speculation and an Oedipal nightmare'. Another work from the same period is called 'Blondes and Brunettes'. Here 16 black and white photographs portray 'Blondes' – in fact all the pictures are from the same girl, with slightly different expressions on her face – and 16 ditto of a 'Brunettes' ditto. This was 'deconstruction' avant la lettre, – examining the important adage that blondes, or brunettes, 'all look alike'.

Wegman became famous for making his dog, 'Man Ray', famous. He photographed Man Ray, a Weimaraner, for 12 years. On the death of this famous model in 1982 THE VILLAGE VOICE ran a full-cover photo of Ray as 'Man of the Year'. A female successor, Fay Ray, made a striking debut at Pace/MacGill Gallery in New York City in December 1987. Among the most impressive portraits shown were those in which Fay posed with Wegman's studio assistant, Andrea L. Beeman, or with the artist Ed Ruscha. Unlike Aesop, Wegman makes his fables with a Polaroid 20 x 24 inches (508 x 610 mm) camera. Like every authentic wit, Wegman's timing is perfect. He also makes it hard to look at conventional portraits without smiling.

STARN TWINS   THE HORSES

Doug and Mike Starn
The Horses No.102, 1986
Toned gelatin-silver prints with Scotch tape,
1015 x 3048 mm
Lent by Eugene and Barbara Schwartz, New York City
The Horses Nos. 1–49
Toned gelatin-silver prints with Scotch tape
By courtesy of Stux Gallery, Boston and New York

'You pick up this little machine and open the shutter just to let in the focused light and you have an image of that time and place and the first place it is transferred to is to a piece of plastic [the negative]. We wanted to bring out that [plastic], we wanted to show it up, so we scratched it.'

Doug Starn

'The tonal and scale variations each image undergoes also play on the instability of memory: photographs are about remembering. The Starns' photographs enact the idea that memory has no fixed state, no ultimate corresponding image, but functions like a fluid that expands and contracts with stress, like the ego.'

Gary Indiana

The Starn Twins are photographic printmakers of positively baroque extravagance. Their tour de force is a series of prints made from one negative of horses' heads. They made 100 variations from this negative – and then threw in No.101 (which measures 1397 x 2743 mm) and No.102 illustrated here. The whole series was made in three weeks as a fundraiser for the Institute of Contemporary Arts, Boston. The Horses' sequence (of which Nos.1 to 49 are also illustrated here) provided 'a dictionary of what we do to an image'. They first hit on this method because they were suddenly deprived of their darkroom, shortly before they had to prepare a show. 'We took prints we had lying around and played with them and all of a sudden that broke everything loose'. The procedure used for some large works is to project a negative onto a wall covered with pieces of positive paper. Each piece of paper is then worked separately in the darkroom. 'We like to see how different toners react to each other, and we are finding more and more ways of scoring prints'. The American tradition of the fine photographic print may have been an irresistible provocation – but there were plenty of precedents available for the kind of work the Starn Twins wanted to do (notably the expansively scored and painted photographic base used by Anselm Kiefer; Julian Schnabel's broken plates).

However, their style and preoccupation with archetypal imagery and their underlying subject of memory – are their own and suggest new areas of exploration by themselves and by others of their generation.

Megan Jenkinson
Five Waters, 1987
Five framed collages exhibited on a shelf
Cibachrome from Polacolor negatives
Each frame 317 x 198 x 64 mm
1. Pacific Water
2. Uranium Sunrise
3. Water of Con/Fusion
4. Plutonium Sunrise
5. Heavy Water
Collection of the Victora & Albert Museum

'New Zealanders are very conscious of our country's place in the Pacific Ocean. In writing about the mythos of islandhood, Behrman, in VICTORIAN MYTHS OF THE SEA, says: "The relationship between the island and the surrounding sea is an intimate one ..." (Behrman is actually referring to the English attitude towards the sea, but it applies equally to our own attitude). In chapter 1 the author also discusses the way that man moulds nature (the sea) to fit his own concepts and theoretical layerings. I discovered this text after making the series but I will quote it here because it is relevant to my way of thinking: "When considering man's relationship to Nature, one is continually struck by how often man forces nature to become an organizing principle for his own perception of reality. He tames the amorphous universe, forcing it to bear the weight of whatever symbolic importance he places on it. Thus the land becomes the garden, the sky the heavens ..." So ... the immensity of the Ocean is contained within a glass ... an amorphous element is organized into a man-made shape.'

Megan Jenkinson, 1988

In retrospect, Megan Jenkinson traces the origin of this series of works to seeing the exhibition 'Art into Production: Soviet Textiles, Fashion and Ceramics, 1917–35' at The Museum of Modern Art, Oxford in 1984. The ceramics particularly impressed her and she found that they were referred to in the catalogue as 'agitational chinaware'. After the October Revolution artists aimed at embodying political and social comment in real, tangible objects – even if, in the event, the masses could not afford finely-crafted porcelain bowls with political slogans in gold-leaf (let alone actually use them). She also recalls reading a dictionary definition of 'Clepsydra', a 'water-clock' or water-glass.

The photographs of water were taken since 1984 off the east coast of New Zealand's North Island. 'Heavy Water' was the first 'Water-Glass' constructed and its name was inspired by the ominous dark-green colour of the water. 'Pacific Water', on the other hand, is a dynamic, upward-spiralling form which represents for the artist 'the sparkling, clear visual quality of Pacific water (OED definition "tending to Peace") – water in its purest form'.

'Five Waters' makes a subtle and indirect comment on the nuclear influence in the Pacific Ocean, and has especial resonance because it is the work of a New Zealand artist. What is most immense – nuclear energy, but also the enormous power of the Pacific Ocean – is allied in these works (by a kind of metaphysical wit) with what is most fragile, with water-glasses based on models of the Renaissance and classical antiquity.

PACIFIC WATER

URANIUM SUNRISE

WATER OF CON/FUSION

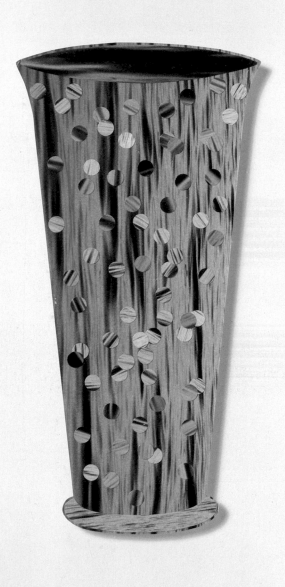

PLUTONIUM SUNSET

HEAVY WATER

MAPPLETHORPE MERCURY

Robert Mapplethorpe
Mercury, 1987
Unique platinum print on linen with cotton fabric and
frame 648 x 1029 mm
Collection of Harry H. Lunn, Jr.

'… critics have complained that his pictures of sex are
too "fashionable" – too polished, too aestheticized –
but fashionability has been one of his biggest crossover
instruments and is among the sharpest devices. By
making his subjects so fashionable, he makes knowledge
of them fashionable instead of something dirty.'

Ingrid Sischy, 1988

'I wasn't setting out to make a statement, that isn't the
way I work. The statement grows out of what I do.'

Robert Mapplethorpe

Platinum is the photographic equivalent of marble. Paper sensitized with platinum salts can, in experienced hands, suggest luminosity within the paper, register an unrivalled tonal range and remain permanently pristine. It is the typical paper of the 25 years up to 1914 and was spectacularly revived by Irving Penn in the 1980s in order to reprint his major contributions to the photography of haute couture from 30 years before.

Robert Mapplethorpe's career as an artist has been concerned with making photographic imagery into objects – into gallery art works – since his beginnings 20 years ago. He has also developed a style of polished elegance which has become as characteristic of our time as Man Ray's solarized photography was of the years around 1930. Most obviously, Mapplethorpe has worked to bring culturally forbidden imagery (racial as well as erotic) into new and visible cultural forms. It is fifteen years since he first explored the relationship of real flesh and its marble parallels in art history.

Mapplethorpe has begun to collect and photograph other Roman sculpture – notably an Apollo, photographed in close-up profile – lips parted – against a black background. Like the Apollo, Mapplethorpe's Mercury is an object of desire – photographed with the sensuousness and panache he had earlier brought to the textures of flowers and living flesh, black and white, male and female.

89 Mercury, 1987

Helen Chadwick
The Oval Court, 1986
Mixed media
Collection of the Victoria & Albert Museum

'In Helen Chadwick's OF MUTABILITY we enter into a post-lapsarian Paradise where woman is visible alone among humankind, where she is the matter in question, but what matters is her passion, her physical articulation of her feelings, her relation to created things and her choice among them; where her aloneness is not an issue and absence not felt, as was the lack of woman felt by Adam. We are introduced into a cycle of experiences, mediated through an imaginary body composed from the artist's own, from photocopies in collage. "I want to catch the physical sensations passing across the body – sensations of gasping, yearning, breathing, fullness," says the artist. "The bodies are bearing their sexuality like a kind of Aeolian harp, through which the sensations are drifting and playing. Each of them is completely swollen up with pleasure at the moment when it's about to turn, each has reached the pitch of plenitude before it starts to decay, to empty …"'.

Marina Warner

'The Oval Court' was part of Helen Chadwick's exhibition at the Institute of Contemporary Arts, London, in 1986 called OF MUTABILITY. This work led to Helen Chadwick being short-listed for the Tate Gallery's Turner Prize in 1987. The citation referred to her 'striking use of mixed media'. These were an office photocopying machine, instant passport photos, a computer (with which Salomonic columns were drawn), and real gold leaf. The general view of the exhibition shows, on the walls, the artist's head (passport photo portraits), from which tears flow down the Salomonic columns to feed a pool in which float 12 figures with emblems, and on which float five gold spheres.

Helen Chadwick chose to use a photocopying machine to represent her nude body and various attributes – fish, flesh, fowl, flora, feathers, fruits. The extremely limited possibilities of the machine yielded images which are at once frankly realistic and curiously mysterious. The machine could only take material of a certain size – not a whole figure, for example – and so fragments were collaged together. Marina Warner wrote in the catalogue of the exhibition:

'The lamb, the skate, the monkfish, the rabbits, the crab, squid, sardines, and the goose which appear to dance and even fly in the embraces of the Lover in the pool have passed into a dreamscape where their existence is no longer actual but only remembered. As Max Friedlander wrote, "Still life can be a symbol of life in flower, or equally it can be the symbol of ruin and death". To stress the sense of transience, Helen Chadwick assembles around the major motifs of these allegorical couples the emblems of further mortification: from the hand of the ecstatic figure whirling with the goose fall maggots from the goose's lights; the double-headed figure of Harvest faces one way to ripeness and bounty, the other towards decomposition; the frivolous ribbons, lacy frills, frothy trailing trimmings and net tights, the schoolgirl socks and other ornaments echo the fripperies of Vanitas paintings. But (in Helen Chadwick's words) "the draperies aren't there as titillating lingerie, but to intensify the decorativeness, because the greater the decoration, the greater the sense of transience. Austerity implies endurance …".'

As Marina Warner makes clear, the inspiration of this work owes much to the artist's visit to the rococo pilgrimage churches of Bavaria. To bring so many sources of inspiration into an authentically new work, using contemporary media, is itself an inspiration.

Woody Vasulka
Art of Memory, 1988
Colour video with sound, 36 minutes
Collection of the Victoria & Albert Museum

'Optically dazzling, Vasulka's high-tech manoeuvres are central to the expression of his theme. Without such technology, his smooth juxtaposition of found footage and New Mexico landscape, of timebound and timeless, and his moving-picture solids would have been virtually impossible. But these are not analogue and digital exercises for their own sake. Here, rather, is an extension in video of the grand ambition of such 19th century painters as Thomas Cole, in his 'Course of Empire' series depicting civilization from dawn to twilight: convincing, "realistic" detail engages the viewer's identification and recollection, while the sublime setting given to it locates human tragedy on a cosmic moral plane.'

Anne H. Hoy

Vasulka has developed visually compelling techniques, which he uses to create an electronic opera based on 20th century history. The setting is the Southwestern landscape of the United States, which symbolizes the grandeur and fragility of the world. The video opens in a red sandstone canyon. A figure on a rock appears to be winged like Icarus. A tourist enters the foreground, snaps the apparition, pauses, then hurls a stone at it. The sky turns to geometric rain. We see newsreel footage of cavalry, blazing buildings, war planes – from revolutions, civil war, world war. The footage is processed into multi-screen, organic shapes abandoned in the desert. We recognise the face and words of Robert J. Oppenheimer, leader of the Manhattan Project which gave America the atomic bomb: 'I remembered a few lines from the Hindu Scripture, the Bhagavad-Gita: "Now I am become death, the destroyer of worlds."' Vasulka's video is like high-speed collage, into which he incorporates documentary film, photographs, slogans, and – most hauntingly – songs. These elements provide the 'opera' with authenticity and a resonance which suggests that we are viewing nothing less than the destiny of the human race in the 20th century, and afterwards. The use of video's advanced technology and editing allow Vasulka the facility of (in his words) 'taking two-dimensional, object-like forms … The image is no longer truth-in-a-window. Truth is subordinate … to this form.' Anne H. Hoy has remarked: 'Vasulka's computer-generated forms convey literally how memory distorts the shape of events, and how permeable is the photograph as a container of supposed truth.' She has also referred to Vasulka's 'investigation of the video signal as a plastic, temporal medium, as electronic energy organized as frequencies, unconfined by the Box (the video "frame").'

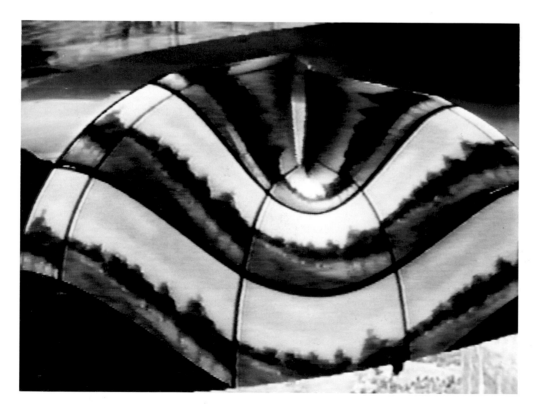

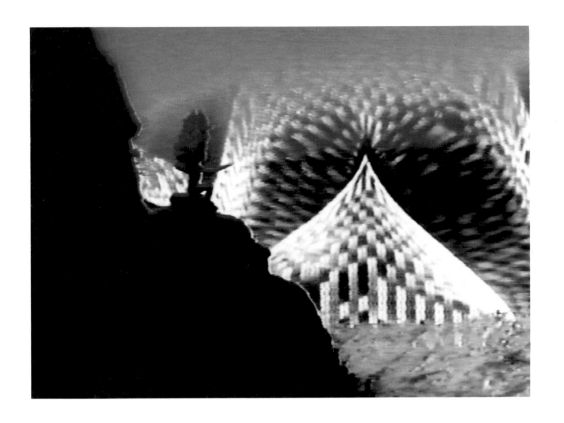

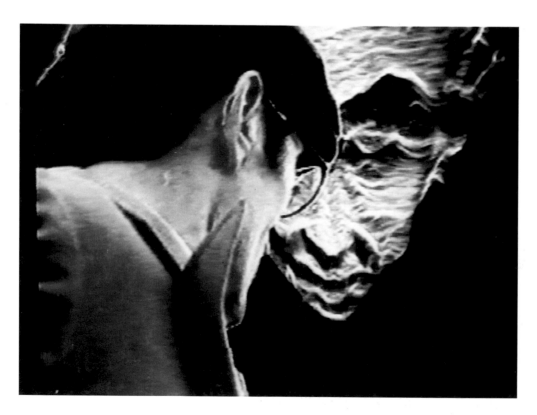

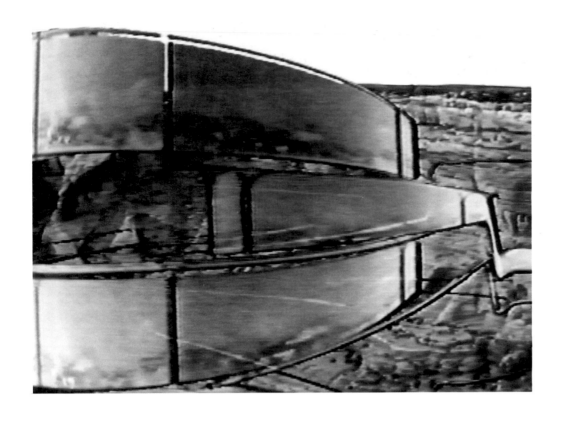

Astrid Klein
Großhirnsalto (Cerebral Somersault), 1984
Gelatin-silver print 2248 x 1270 mm
Collection of the Victoria & Albert Museum

Astrid Klein was trained at art school but began as a writer. Her universe is informed by the writings of, among others, Kafka, Artaud, Beckett. She made photoworks which combine newspaper images with text in the late 1970s. At that date the subject-matter of the photographs was perfectly legible and the works gained their force and content from the way two or more photographs were placed side by side: a woman's face in close-up, an ominous highway at night. By 1981 the artist was using photographic imagery as if it was purely graphic material, as if the literal meanings had been dissolved in a solution of ideas and metaphors – except that the half-tone dots from newsprint were emphatically part of the image. Nightmares were validated, like facts. She speaks of art as 'needles for the brain'.

Klein uses photographs from newspapers and magazines or taken by herself. She uses such techniques as 'sandwiching' negatives in the enlarger. She makes negative prints and she manipulates photographic materials with acid. Exceptionally among artists using photography, she uses 'plastic' – resin-coated – paper for printing. It has a pallor not only appropriate to her imagery but necessary to it. Her work belongs in the awesome tradition of German graphic art but also has the chilling grandeur of the paintings of Francis Bacon.

The imagery of 'Cerebral Somersault' is familiar and also strange. Several elements are mixed, held together in solution, in the picture and in an observer's mind: motifs reminiscent of radiation warnings and computer technology, of the human afterimages left at Hiroshima, of effigies from ancient times or an imminent future, of graves and hard rain. Catastrophe is the principal subject of much of the significant art of the present, but few artists have been able to synthesise imagery of this order of resonance. Astrid Klein's work addresses the imagination – not the slogan-reading part of the brain – because, in her words, 'if the danger is inside, it can be reached in no other way'.

101 Großhirnsalto (Cerebral Somersault), 1984

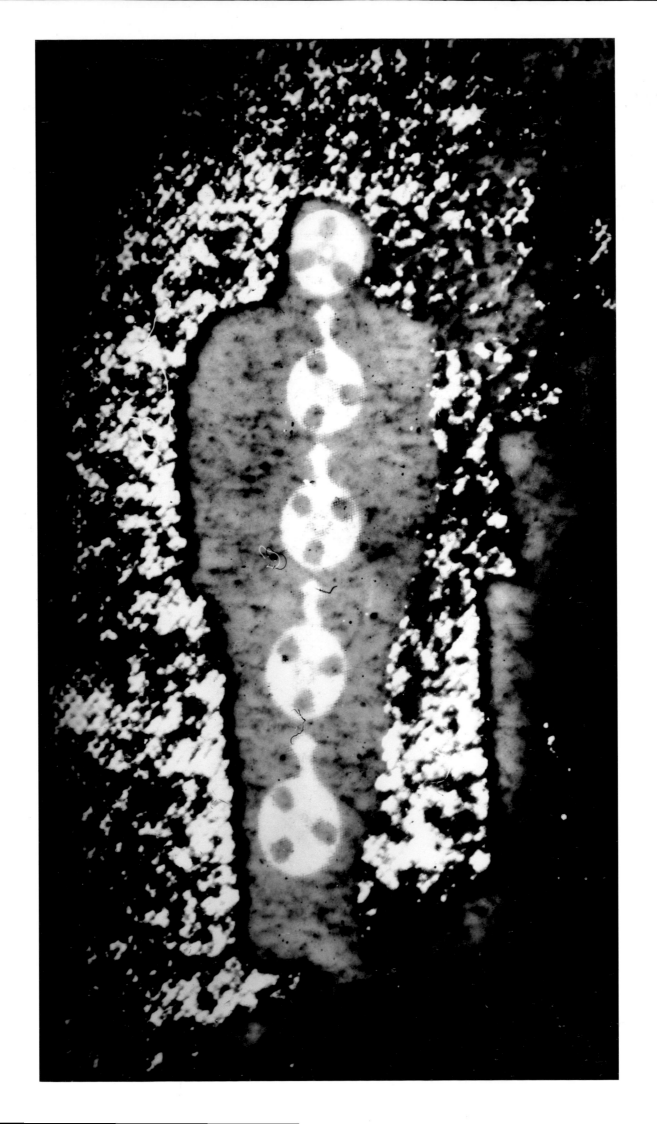

FUKASE RAVENS

Masahisa Fukase
Ravens
A series of photographs made in the years 1975–86,
published in book form in 1986
The prints in the Victoria & Albert Museum Collection
measure 279 x 355 mm and 762 x 1016 mm
Collection of the Victoria & Albert Museum

Fukase's series RAVENS preoccupied him for ten years, beginning with a chance photograph of a flock of crows on his native Hokkaido in 1975 and culminating in the publication of 62 photographs in 1986. Crows or Ravens? Perhaps the series includes both species and is about the genus Crow and its symbolic properties. The first photographs on the theme, taken in a burst of activity in 1975–78, were part of another long and complex work. Fukase's wife Yohko inspired a whole narrative cycle, eventually published in 1978, in which parts of the Crow/Ravens series play an ominous role. Yohko was a Noh performer and the work, essentially dramatic in its juxtapositions, staging and sequencing, was derived from their marriage and, in 1976, their divorce. Many of the photographs of birds are profoundly melancholic. A quality of obsession and loss links photographs in the series – the black wings of a girl's hair, the flying debris of a Tokyo rubbish tip, black shapes in the sky like a wave of planes. The series is exceptional in two ways: first the sheer graphic invention with which Fukase describes and interprets the birds. Mark Holborn has written: 'The silver eye and black silhouette were photographed in a similar convention to sumi-e ink painting, like brush strokes in the sky'. A similar graphic intensity and inventiveness can be found in two of Fukase's great contemporaries in Tokyo, Eikoh Hosoe and Daido Moriyama. Like them, Fukase also has the ability to link imagery in a complicated sequence, so that a great number of disparate subjects can be – surprisingly – unified. The photographs are linked across the book by fleeting resemblances, oppositions, repetitions, the pictorial equivalents of assonance and half-rhyme.

FRIEDLANDER   CHERRY BLOSSOM TIME IN JAPAN

Lee Friedlander
Cherry Blossom Time in Japan, 1986
Photogravures printed by Thomas Palmer
Typography by Katy Homans
Binding by George Wieck
Calligraphy by Shuntei Taniguchi
Published in an edition of 50 copies plus six artists'
copies by Haywire Press, New City, New York
25 photogravure prints, each measuring approximately
8½ x 12¾ inches (216 x 324mm) on sheets measuring
15 x 20½ inches (381 x 520 mm)
Collection of the Victoria & Albert Museum
By courtesy of Zabriskie Gallery, New York

Photogravure came into commercial use about 1880. It was a development of a photomechanical printing process invented by W. H. F. Talbot in 1858, as improved by Karel Klic. It was used for postcards, art reproductions and by photographic artists – like Peter Henry Emerson – for making fine, limited edition books and portfolios. Photogravure was much in use during the Photo-Secession period in the early years of the 20th century – a time of intense seriousness about photography as a vehicle of genuine graphic art and of intense interest in Japanese aesthetics. The process fell into gradual disuse between the wars but has, like many earlier processes, been revived in the last few years. A bright, tack-sharp surface has characterised much of the excellent photography of our era but in his book FLOWERS AND TREES (1981) Friedlander chose a flat, grey tonality that recalled the mild, understated landscape photography of the early part of the century. Photogravure, with its softer outlines, seemed an appropriate printing method for his Japanese portfolio. Many of his compositions play with the merging of foreground, middle-distance and background details into one overlapping pattern. He also plays with the notion that the form of a bridge derives from the form of a pine branch and the soft gradations of the photogravure process helps to merge these two forms. The process also places the series of photographs, taken in Japan between 1977 and 1984, at a remove from the present, as if this is the album of an early 20th century visitor to an exotic country whose ideas concerning nature and culture were so profoundly attractive to the West.

108 Kyoto 1977
109 Kyoto 1977
110 Tokyo 1974

Dieter Appelt
Canto, 1981–86
Calotype
Ezra Pound, 1981–86
Platinum print and negative gelatin-silver print
By courtesy of the
Kicken-Pauseback Galerie, Cologne
Ezra Pound, 1981–86
Platinum print, calotype and negative gelatin-silver print
By courtesy of the
Kicken-Pauseback Galerie, Cologne

Dieter Appelt uses his own body in much of his photographic work – sometimes simply his own hands, or face. He began a sequence titled EZRA POUND in 1981. He was deeply impressed by a line in Pound's PISAN CANTOS:
'A lizard upheld me
the wild birds would not eat the white bread'.

The work was centred on the PISAN CANTOS, which were written when Pound was imprisoned after his arrest on treason charges (for broadcasting in favour of the Fascist cause on Italian radio). Appelt visited Pisa, Rapallo and Venice and made some 40 photographs on the Pound theme. He reconstructed some photographs of Pound in Venice, using himself as model. In one of these reconstructions he wears Pound's overcoat. He photographed the room in which the poet died (in 1972) using an exposure time of many hours and making a negative print. He was unable to print some negatives as he wished to until he discovered the possibilities offered by the earlier, historical processes. He visited W. H. F. Talbot's house and museum at Lacock Abbey, Wiltshire, in the summer of 1987 and immediately experimented with Talbot's calotype process and then learned how to make platinum prints. He found that some of his Pound negatives could only be printed effectively with platinum paper, which has a very long tonal range. This kind of paper, in use in the 25 years up to 1914 but revived in recent times, also places the EZRA POUND photographs in a time outside the present – suggesting, perhaps a vision of Venice in the time of the "Belle Epoque" when Pound first came to Europe as a young man and revolutionized poetics in the English language. Appelt successfully utilizes the characteristics of platinum printing and negative printing as part of his interpretation of – and homage to – Ezra Pound.

112 From CANTO, 1981–86

113

113 From EZRA POUND, 1981–86

114

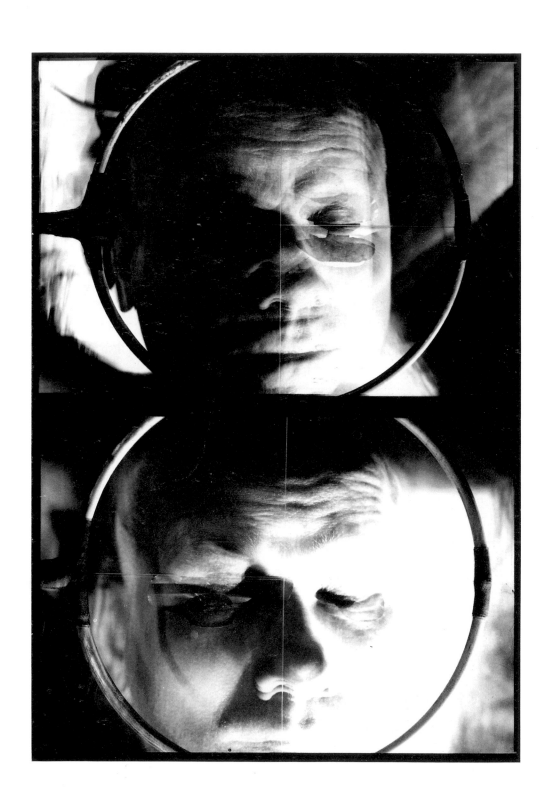

PHOTOGRAPHY BOOKS

William Henry Fox Talbot
THE PENCIL OF NATURE 1844–46
A limited edition facsimile of 250 sets, 297 x 233 mm
Commentary by Larry J. Schaaf, research and production
by Larry J. Schaaf and Hans P. Kraus, Jr., printing and
binding by Martino Mardersteig, Stamperia Valdonega,
Verona, Italy. Tri-tone negative separation
by Robert J. Hennessey.
Published by Hans P. Kraus, Jr., Inc., New York City on 25
January 1989.
Collection of the Victoria & Albert Museum

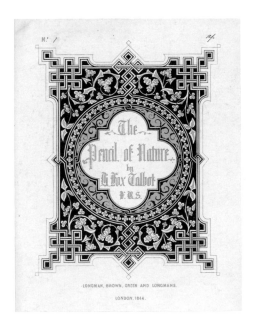

Henry Talbot, the British inventor of the positive/negative process of photography, first publicly showed examples of an earlier phase of his invention – which he called Photogenic Drawing – at the Royal Institution in London on 25 January 1839. His invention of photogenic drawing dated back four years earlier but he was spurred to bring it to the attention of the scientific world by the announcement by the Frenchman Daguerre of his revolutionary invention, the Daguerreotype. Daguerre prevailed in the early years but the future belonged to positive/negative photography and to Talbot. THE PENCIL OF NATURE was Talbot's attempt to acquaint the general public with the characteristics and scope of his process, which in 1841 he had decisively improved (and called the Calotype). THE PENCIL OF NATURE was published in six parts between June 1844 and April 1846. It is the first commercially published book illustrated by photography. Talbot wrote texts which described the plates and what they exemplify. The plates, original calotypes, were printed by Talbot's assistants at what was called The Reading Establishment. Time has taken its toll of the copies produced in the 1840s. Hans P. Kraus and Larry J. Schaaf conducted a census of surviving copies in 1986–88 and discovered that fewer than 40 sets survived. For this facsimile edition they have chosen the best preserved prints from each set as the basis for reproduction – thus creating a best-possible edition, as well as preserving Talbot's work for future times. Every aspect of Talbot's original has been closely studied and painstakingly reconstructed. Talbot's prints are found in many different colours and these have been rendered in the new prints. A scholarly text by Schaaf throws much new light on Talbot's work.

Pierre Apraxine and Richard Benson
PHOTOGRAPHS FROM THE COLLECTION OF THE GILMAN
PAPER COMPANY
A book of 478 pages with 199 plates, 458 x 390 mm
Printing by Richard Benson
Text printing by Stamperia Valdonega, Verona, Italy
Foreword by Howard Gilman, Introduction by Pierre
Apraxine, Notes by Lee Marks, Afterword by Richard
Benson
White Oak Press, New York 1985
Collection of the Victoria & Albert Museum

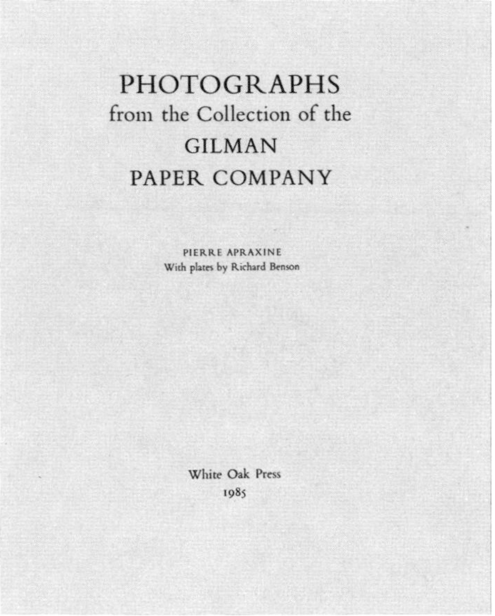

This book is among the great monuments of photographic effort and achievement in the 1980s. The volume represents what can be done by the unified efforts of a corporation, a curator and a printer. The company is active in conservation, tree genetics, education and – since 1974 – art collecting. Gilman's became the most impressive corporate collection of photographs ever assembled (although mention should be made of the special achievement of the Canadian Centre for Architecture) – but what is even more remarkable is the way the riches of the collection have been translated into the facsimile plates in this book, and thus into the great libraries of the world and the public domain. (In fact travelling exhibitions of these plates, selected by Bruce Bernard, are circulating in the UK under the auspices of the South Bank Board). The plates were printed by Richard Benson, assisted by Thomas Palmer, using a Meihle 29 inch, single colour offset press. Each plate was printed separately, sometimes with as many as nine passes through the press. 200,000 separate prints were made. Richard Benson wrote of the method he evolved: 'For years I have loved the broad and smooth areas of colour that exist in posters printed by stone lithography, and in working with the halftone screen to reproduce photographs, I have struggled to apply this inherently lithographic quality to the work of the stone's descendant, the modern offset press .... In each reproduction of this book there is at least one solid layer of ink, with no half-tone dot, running through most of the tones of the picture. This lends a density and structure to the plates not usually associated with photo-offset lithography' (Afterword).

PHOTOGRAPHS
from the Collection of the
GILMAN
PAPER COMPANY

PIERRE APRAXINE
With plates by Richard Benson

White Oak Press
1985

John Szarkowski and Maria Morris Hambourg
THE WORK OF ATGET 1981–85
Four volumes, each 298 x 257 mm.
Volume I: Old France 1981; 180 pages, 121 tritone plates, 83 reference illustrations
Volume II: The Art of Old Paris 1982; 192 pages, 117 tritone plates, 95 reference illustrations
Volume III: The Ancien Regime 1983; 180 pages, 120 tritone plates, 47 reference illustrations
Volume IV: Modern Times 1985; 183 pages, 116 tritone plates, 89 reference illustrations
Printed by Meriden Gravure, Meriden, Connecticut, USA
Part of Springs Industries Series on the Art of Photography
Published by The Museum of Modern Art, New York, and Gordon Fraser, London

In 1968 The Museum of Modern Art, New York, acquired a collection of some 5000 prints and plates by the French photographer Eugene Atget (1857–1927). These had been purchased from Atget's estate in 1928 by the American photographer Berenice Abbott, then a pupil of Man Ray. Under its director, John Szarkowski, The Department of Photography at The Museum of Modern Art organized, studied and catalogued the collection. In 1976 Maria Morris Hambourg began to study the collection and Atget's life and work and in 1980 completed her doctoral dissertation 'Eugene Atget, 1857–1927: The Structure of the Work' (Columbia University). The four volumes elucidate problems of dating, structure and interpretation in Atget's work and make clear the centrality of his achievement to many of the later concerns of photographic artists. Thanks to a subvention from Springs Mills, Inc., The Museum of Modern Art was able to publish Atget's photographs with a rare degree of authenticity. John Szarkowski wrote in the preface to the first volume: 'Atget's own prints were made over a period of many years, on a variety of photographic papers. Many of these prints have shifted subtly in colour or tonality, in ways more apparent to the lithographer's camera than to our own eyes. This factor has exacerbated the already extremely difficult problem of translating into a screened image the sense of the photograph's continuous tone.' He went on to commend the interpretive skills of Richard Benson, who made the halftone negatives and worked closely with the craftsmen at Meriden Gravure in Meriden, Connecticut, who printed the plates in tritone (which involves making three negatives – for light, dark and middle tones – for each print, and two passes through the press). Such publications as THE WORK OF ATGET have set an international standard in the 1980s. The Museum of Modern Art has also been able to give contemporary photographic artists catalogues published to a standard possibly even higher than that achieved with the Atget volumes: see, for example, NICHOLAS NIXON: PICTURES OF PEOPLE, printed in tritone by Franklin Graphics, Providence, Rhode Island, 1988.

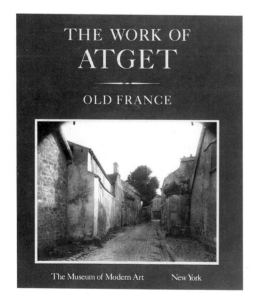

PHOTO POCHE

A series of booklets
190 x 125 mm
Published by the Centre National de la Photographie
with the aid of the Ministère de la Culture et de la
Communication, Paris.
Series directed by Robert Delpire, director of the Centre
National de la Photographie.
Collection of the National Art Library,
Victoria & Albert Museum.

The aim of this series, which now numbers over 35 titles, is to provide a collection of carefully printed, cheap, pocket-sized photo books which offer introductions to the major themes of the medium and to a number of its key individuals. Some of the books have been translated and are marketed in the USA by Pantheon Books. The use of quality printing (in duotone) is unusual and impressive at this format, as is the variety of topics covered.

Another important initiative by this French government agency includes its support for a series of television films made by the distinguished director Agnes Varda. These programmes, which last one minute each and deal with one photograph each, are called 'Une Minute Pour Une Image'. 365 films were made; they were broadcast on French television.

In the field of popularisation, several other series of books should be mentioned: the History of Photography series published by Aperture, New York; the Lucida series published in Helsingborg, Sweden; the Photo-Library series by Dirk Nishen Publishing in Berlin and London, and the series Colección Rió de Luz on Mexican photographers edited by Pedro Meyer and published by the Fondo de Cultura Económica in Mexico City. These publishing initiatives have served simultaneously to define a photographic heritage particular to each country and to familiarise a young audience with a wide range of historical materials and expressive styles.

Richard Avedon
IN THE AMERICAN WEST, 1979–84 (1985)
A book of 184 pages, with 120 plates printed in duotone
363 x 285 mm
Printing by Dai Nippon, Japan
Design by Marvin Israel and Elizabeth Avedon
Foreword by Richard Avedon
Background by Laura Wilson
Published by Harry N. Abrams, New York and Thames and Hudson, London
Collection of the Victoria & Albert Museum

'A portrait photographer depends upon another person to complete his picture. The subject imagined, which in a sense is me, must be discovered in someone else willing to take part in a fiction he cannot possibly know about. My concerns are not his. We have separate ambitions for the image. His need to plead his case probably goes as deep as my need to plead mine, but the control is with me.

A portrait is not a likeness. The moment an emotion or fact is transformed into a photograph it is no longer a fact but an opinion. There is no such thing as inaccuracy in a photograph. All photographs are accurate. None of them is the truth.'

Richard Avedon

This is the most handsomely designed and arresting photographic book of the 1980s. It was the last of Richard Avedon's books to be designed by Marvin Israel, his close associate on many projects, who worked in close collaboration with Elizabeth Avedon (daughter-in-law of the photographer). Like Richard Avedon, Marvin Israel was a pupil of Alexey Brodovitch. Israel designed Avedon's PORTRAITS (1976) and two of his most important exhibitions: JACOB ISRAEL AVEDON at the Museum of Modern Art, New York (1974) and a sensational exhibition of large-scale prints at the Marlborough Gallery in New York (1975). He also designed another epoch-making book, DIANE ARBUS (1972), as well as pursuing an influential career as art director at HARPER'S BAZAAR. Elizabeth Avedon designed Avedon's PHOTO-GRAPHS 1947–1977 and the exhibition of the same title shown at the Metropolitan Museum of Art, New York in 1978. The brilliance of the book design is matched by the virtuosity of the printing by Dai Nippon. Although they had already proved their skills with other publications, this book probably did most to signal the arrival of the Japanese as major quality printers in western markets. The style of the book is almost cinematic, with images unfolding before the viewer reads the 'titles', as if to bear out Avedon's remark 'I don't think the West of these portraits is any more conclusive than the West of John Wayne'. Six summers of work were initiated by a commission from the Amon Carter Museum of Western Art in Fort Worth, Texas, to make an interpretation and record of the region through portraiture. Working with assistants, and his usual 8 x 10 inch Deardorf camera, Avedon made a total of 17,000 portraits of 732 people in 189 locations in 17 states. He worked out of doors, with natural light and a white background. Reflector boards shone light up into the subjects' faces to refine the modelling (reflections give a certain hooded look to the eyes in the portrait here). The prints in the accompanying exhibition were also of epic proportion – some five feet by four and even larger.

The Rattlesnake Round-up in Sweetwater, Texas, takes place every March to rid rangeland of snakes and make it safer for livestock. The portrait of Boyd Fortin was the first in Avedon's project and in some ways set the tone and style of what was to come, linking the Western portraits to previous preoccupations. There were three sessions over two days. The portrait is hyper-real, with almost obsessive attention to surface, to clothing. The face is that of a Renaissance choirboy, or cupid, caught up in some act of Southern atavism. He holds not only a gutted Diamond-back but a pose ordained as well as caught by the photographer. The isolation of the portrait appears to be a statement about a society – and a photographer. Avedon used the same mixture of innocence and repellant physicality in a notorious portrait two years later of the young actress Nastassia Kinski posing naked with a python.

121 From IN THE AMERICAN WEST, 1979–84
Boyd Fortin, thirteen years old,
Sweetwater, Texas, 10 March 1979
59 5/8 x 47 1/8 in
© Richard Avedon

TSUCHIDA   HIROSHIMA

Hiromi Tsuchida
HIROSHIMA (1985)
A book of 204 pages, 142 plates, 277 x 260 mm
Printed by offset lithography in Japan
Book design by Kazuo Nitta
Text in Japanese and English
Published by Kosei Publishing, Tokyo
Collection of the Victoria & Albert Museum

This book has three parts: 'Hiroshima Monument' is a series of photographs taken between 1979 and 1983 which is introduced as follows. 'In the city of Hiroshima a few things, such as trees, bridges, and buildings, survived the bombing and stand unobtrusively, but not forgotten, among the many new buildings'. On each left hand page, facing each of the photographs, is a street plan of the centre of Hiroshima. A star marks the epicentre of the atomic bomb dropped in 1945. Concentric circles indicate distances 1 km, 2 km and 3 km from the epicentre. A dot indicates where the photograph on the right hand page was taken. Quite ordinary buildings - a Kirin beer hall built in the 1930s, for example - or a small stand of camphor trees, survived at a distance of only 700 metres from the epicentre. The book simultaneously conveys an appreciation of the intricacy of what is left and how the smallest scraps surviving from before 1945 possess the stature of monuments - and indicates the depth of the trauma produced by the events of 1945. The second section, 'Hiroshima 1945-1979', is a set of portraits of contributors to 'Genbaku no ko' (Children of the Atomic Bombing), 186 accounts by children of what happened to them on 6 August 1945. Their words, first published in 1951, are quoted in the book beside portraits made some 30 years later (1976-79). The third part, 'Hiroshima Collection', is a meticulously photographed series of artefacts from the 6,600 articles gathered together in the Hiroshima Peace Memorial Museum.

ピロシマ

Hiroshima 土田ヒロミ Hiromi Tsuchida

123 From HIROSHIMA, plate 15
Pine tree, Sumiyoshi shrine, 1,400 metres
from the epicentre

John R. Gossage
THE POND (1985)
A book of 49 photographs, unnumbered pages,
280 x 300 mm
Design by Gabriele F. Götz and John R. Gossage
Cover photograph printed by John R. Gossage
Duotone plates by O. R. T., Berlin
Printed by offset lithography by Brüder Hartmann,
Berlin
Essay by Denise Sines
Published by Aperture, New York 1985

There are close relationships of style and preoccupation between this book and LOS ANGELES SPRING by Robert Adams, SAN QUENTIN POINT by Lewis Baltz, and WAFFENRUHE by Michael Schmidt. The passionate understatement of Hiromi Tsuchida's HIROSHIMA also appears to be related to a movement which has become international – that first identified by the exhibition NEW TOPOGRAPHICS: PHOTO-GRAPHS OF A MAN-ALTERED LANDSCAPE (International Museum of Photography, George Eastman House, NY 1975). Among the characteristics of the new landscape photography is its willingness to extend the idea of what landscape IS. The 'social landscape' ignores the preference for peaks in national parks. It also mounts a large-scale critique of the human management of the environment. The manner in which this is done, however, can be quizzical and unexpected as in Gossage's book THE POND. This sequence of photographs is arranged like a walk in a locality familiar to the photographer and, in some similar form, to any townsman or villager. It could be likened to a carefully positioned set of film stills. The intervals between the spots where the photographer paused to photograph can be filled with the viewer's own narrative material, or memories. The photographer's glance alights on small details of foliage or suddenly sweeps upwards to the open sky. Despite the occasional drabness of the place, there is an alacrity of attention to intricacies, that makes the book unlike any other. The photographs are an act of reclamation of a kind of urban territory that long ago stopped being land-scape. They represent a reassuring urban parallel to the exotic exploits of Richard Long and Hamish Fulton.

125 From THE POND, plate 40
Mount Ranier, Maryland
By courtesy of Castelli Graphics, New York

Robert Adams
LOS ANGELES SPRING: PHOTOGRAPHS BY ROBERT ADAMS
(1986)
A book of 50 photographs, 242 x 305 mm
Printed in 300-line screen duotone offset
lithography by Stamperia Valdonega, Verona
Negatives by Robert Hennessey
Published by Aperture, New York

'Whether those trees that stand are reassuring is a question for a lifetime. All that is clear is the perfection of what we were given, the unworthiness of our response, and the certainty, in view of our current deprivation, that we are judged.'

Robert Adams

Robert Adams has photographed subjects which have usually been ignored by photographers driving somewhere else, to where landscape really begins. His vision of American places is both shockingly ordinary and pristine, like something never before focused on. That is certainly true of his book FROM THE MISSOURI WEST (Aperture, 1980). Instead of taking up the normal position from which to look at Los Angeles – which would be that of a driver – Adams adopts the role of a botanist, or perhaps a botanical historian looking for traces of the Eden that Southern California is well attested to have been 80 years ago: 'live oaks on the hills, orchards across the valleys, and ornamental cypress, palms, and eucalyptus lining the roads'. LOS ANGELES SPRING is a book of photographs of trees. It seems doubtful that any other photographer has given so much attention to the condition of trees growing in close proximity to urban man. As the book unfolds, the condition of trees becomes an index of or a metaphor for the health of the surrounding culture.

127 From LOS ANGELES SPRING, plate 12
Overlooking Long Beach
By Courtesy of Fraenkel Gallery, San Francisco

Lewis Baltz
SAN QUENTIN POINT (1986)
A book of 58 plates, unnumbered pages, 268 x 278 mm
Duotone by O. R. T., Berlin
Printing by Brüder Hartmann, Berlin
Design by Gabriele F. Götz and Lewis Baltz
Essay by Mark Haworth-Booth
Published by Aperture, New York in association with
Verlag Zwölftes Haus, Berlin

'By means of the camera's viewfinder, the outside world goes through a process of selection and organization. Things become pertinent; thanks to the parameters of the frame, they take shape in relation to vertical and horizontal limits. We know at once what is good and what is bad. Like the microscope, the frame is an analyzing tool.'

Nestor Almendros, from MAN WITH A CAMERA

San Quentin Point is the third part of a trilogy which began with THE NEW INDUSTRIAL PARKS NEAR IRVINE, CALIFORNIA (1975) – a foundation block of the 'New Topographics' – and was followed by PARK CITY, a book of 102 photographs which describe the construction of a ski resort of that name a few miles east of Salt Lake City, Utah (published 1980). Marvin Heiferman's phrase 'Landscape-as-Real-Estate' is apt for much of Lewis Baltz's trilogy. SAN QUENTIN POINT was photographed on waste ground close to what Baltz has described as 'the most notoriously affluent and bourgeois suburban county in California'. The prison kept speculation at arm's length for years, but now luxury apartment blocks, boutiques and parking lots prevail. The book contains 58 photographs of this unprepossessing site. To what end? A 'Waste Land', in Eliot's sense, to begin with. Something seen with the perfect frankness and actual ambiguity of the camera, also. To brood on the unkempt surface of the earth as Baltz has done is to find that normal ideas of scale are suspended. Some of these pictures are like electron microscope photographs of skin, or like space shots of the Badlands. Baltz uses the camera like a microscope and his pictures suggest that the disturbances observed here in miniature are legible as part of a larger allegory. He observes a set of violations set in a microcosm and the photographs resonate with an irony reminiscent of the manner in which the behaviour of Lilliputians was chronicled by Jonathan Swift. At a certain age many children wander among disregarded places like San Quentin Point, picking their way through the rubble of the adult world. It is unlikely that anyone could be sentimental about such places – or ever quite unlock their hold on a distant stratum of the imagination.

129 From SAN QUENTIN POINT, no. 52 (and cover)
By courtesy of Castelli Graphics, New York

John R. Gossage
STADT DES SCHWARZ:
EIGHTEEN PHOTOGRAPHS OF BERLIN (1987)
A book of 24 pages with 10 plates, 460 x 338 mm
Design and coordination by Gabriele F. Götz, Ulrich
Görlich and John R. Gossage
Duotone plates by O. R. T., Berlin
Printing by Brüder Hartmann, Berlin
Printing of cover photograph by John R. Gossage
Published by Loosestrife Editions, Washington, DC
in an edition of 500 copies
Introduction by Jane Livingston and three legends based
on the collection of Jacob and Wilhelm Grimm: 'The
Nightmare', 'Cursed to Remain Standing', 'The Crack
Shot'

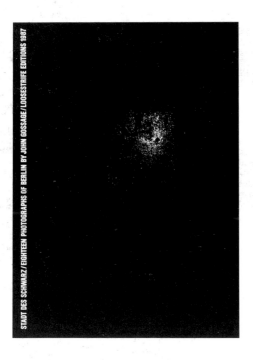

Night photography was a speciality of the 1930s and resulted in remarkable books like Brassai's PARIS DE NUIT (1933) and Bill Brandt's A NIGHT IN LONDON (1938). Gossage's images of Berlin at night, and as a black city, are reminiscent of photographs taken 50 years ago and resonate with a sense of Berlin's history. The photographs are also persuasive evocations of the divided Berlin of the present, where East and West meet beside a floodlit No Man's Land. Gossage made the photographs on visits to Berlin between 1982 and 1986. Each plate in the book is over 381 x 305 mm in size and the printing is a technical tour de force. The tales from Grimm add another dimension to the book. One tells of Drud, or Nightmare, familiar in folk-tale, another tells of an uncanny, supernatural instance: a master gunsmith could hit anything in range of his rifle even if he could not see the object. He fires into the night and kills the enemy, 'sitting on his horse, casually eating his dinner', thus saving the city. A third story details a long punishment in which a child – like parts of Berlin to this day – is compelled to stand absolutely still.

The book manages to bring together some of the special sensations of vision at night, a sense of Berlin's unique and disturbing atmosphere, and an imagery derived from folktale.

131 From STADT DES SCHWARZ, unnumbered plates
Niederkirchnerstraße. Richtung Osten blickend
By courtesy of Castelli Graphics, New York

Michael Schmidt
WAFFENRUHE (1987)
A book of 39 photographs, unnumbered pages,
300 x 265 mm
Duotone plates by O. R. T. Kirchner+Graser, Berlin
Printing by Heenemann, Berlin
Text by Einar Schleef, with a note by Janos Frecot
Published by the Photography Collection of the
Berlinische Galerie in association with Verlag Dirk
Nishen, Berlin

'If we ask the same question of WAFFENRUHE that we asked of Schmidt's earlier documentary works: "Is Berlin really like this?" the most appropriate answer would be: "It is now".'

Lewis Baltz

'Waffenruhe' translates as truce, armistice, an uneasy, provisional peace. What is Berlin like in the late 1980s? It is like these photographs and, as Lewis Baltz has written in a review of the book:

'London, Paris, and Rome have histories, but Berlin has a past. It is the Sodom of our century, destroyed for her sins and then left as a stern reminder. Since the 1920s Berlin has been a city encountered through images: Döblin, Pabst and Isherwood; the diabolic glamour of Nazism; Year Zero; the Airlift; John Kennedy, and spies coming in from the cold; the generation of '68, the stylized desperation of the punk underground, and angels made corporeal. These are some of the images that make the myth. But myths do not exist only to give human proportions to events; they are also created to mystify experience. Mythic images may be the ones to distrust most. Yet the idea of a post-apocalyptic city captivates the contemporary mind and its images continue to proliferate. Soon Berlin will become overpopulated by images, like New York and Paris, and its images will have lost their powers, save those of reflecting and recalling one another.' (From 'Notes on WAFFENRUHE', published in German translation in CAMERA AUSTRIA, no.26, 1988).

A 'post-apocalyptic city' – Schmidt's work shares a vision of past-and-future-catastrophe with contemporaries including, in England, Chris Killip, and – in a different style entirely – Astrid Klein. Schmidt's work in his book BERLIN-WEDDING (1978), photographed in a grey, reflected light, evoked an atmosphere of sterility, uniformity and blight. As Lewis Baltz also noted, there has been a characteristic of 'No-light' in much German photography since the work of Bernd and Hilla Becher in the 1960s. Schmidt's prints, and the plates in his book, possess a drained pallor. His handling of the camera is also drained of the documentary information of his earlier work, but it has possibly become more truthful as an interpretation of Berlin.

133 From WAFFENRUHE, p.55, p.77, p.17, Triptychon

Lynne Cohen
OCCUPIED TERRITORY (1987)
A book of 112 pages, with 88 plates monochrome,
227 x 285 mm
Printed by offset lithography in Hong Kong
Edited and designed by William A. Ewing
Texts by David Byrne and David Mellor
Published by Aperture, New York

David Byrne wrote the perfect introduction to Lynne Cohen's book, which needs to be a book because the evidence has to accumulate to a certain point to become interesting (and unforgettable):

'The photos are probably indistinguishable from those used in annual reports, medical textbooks, and catalogues of technical supplies. Cohen's photos are taken from the same dumb angle. It's the kind of angle that makes us look at the space of the room that's being photographed and the arrangement of objects in the room rather than the subjective viewpoint of the picture taker – recalling the very beginnings of photography when it was a simple recording device, and before it was considered a means of expression, when it sometimes didn't strive to imitate painting. Cohen intrudes as little as possible, thereby leaving the subject being photographed free of "contamination". This objective consideration allows the viewer to add his/her "art appreciation" to these places ... to "complete" the work. It's more satisfying and exciting to add the art yourself than being told how to look or feel about something. Through simple framing and neutral observation these environments appear as a strange, exciting kind of art. It could be high-tech folk art. In fact, it seems that the best modern art exhibitions are going on out there in various institutions and building lobbies ....

The aesthetic evidenced in these rooms has also brought us to the brink of World War III. It's beautiful, it's efficient, it's terrifying, it's funny. THIS is the flowering of our civilization, not Monet's waterlilies, which now seem like a remnant of a prehistoric way of thinking. Oddly enough the waterlilies are displayed in rooms remarkably similar to these.'

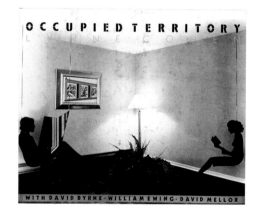

135 From OCCUPIED TERRITORY, p.65: 'Model Living Room'
By courtesy of PPOW Gallery, New York, and Interim Art,
London.

Aperture
Number 98, Spring 1985, 'Western Spaces'
A magazine of 79 pages, 62 illustrations in black and white and colour, plus cover, 290 x 244 mm
Duotone printing by Meriden Gravure, Inc.; Colour separation by L. S. Graphic, Inc., New York; Colour printing by D. L. Terwilliger Co., New York
Executive Director, Michael E. Hoffman; Editor, Mark Holborn; Managing Editor, Larry Frascella; Production Consultant, Steve Baron; Designer, Wendy Byrne.
Published by Aperture, a division of Silver Mountain Foundation, Inc., New York.

Magazines are very seldom reviewed but we depend on them for up to date information. APERTURE was founded in 1952 by some of the most distinguished names in American photographic history: Minor White, Dorothea Lange, Nancy Newhall, Ansel Adams, Beaumont Newhall, Barbara Morgan, Ernest Louis, Melton Ferris and Dody Warren. The magazine became and remains perhaps the most important forum for the publication of outstanding new photography from around the world. Design and production standards are impressively high. The magazine is quarterly and in recent years has devoted each issue to a focused topic. APERTURE No.98, 'Western Spaces', addressed landscape, bringing together a critical article by Lewis Baltz on the CALIFORNIA LANDSCAPES of Edward Weston, an essay by Robert Adams on the legacy from the nineteenth century pioneers of landscape photography in the United States, and selections of photographs by David Avison, Richard Misrach, Art Sinsabaugh, William Clift, Frank Gohlke, Robert Adams, Edward Ranney, Lawrence McFarland, Mark Klett – including his work for the 'Rephotographic Survey' undertaken by the University of New Mexico, Marilyn Bridges, Terry Husebye, David Hockney, NASA and Emmet Gowin (a strikingly different interpretation of Mount St. Helen's from Frank Gohlke's). This issue alone makes clear how much distinguished photographic work has necessarily been ommitted from PHOTOGRAPHY NOW. Other magazines which actively promote a wide range of important new photography include CREATIVE CAMERA, London, PICTURE SHOW, Stockholm, PERSPEKTIEF, Rotterdam, CAMERA AUSTRIA, Graz, THE MANIPULATOR, Hamburg, PHOTO-VISION, Madrid, EUROPEAN PHOTOGRAPHY, Göttingen.

Apart from their vital role in the present, much of the photographic history written in future times will be based on these magazines.

Cover of APERTURE No.98, 'Western Spaces'
Cover photo by Mark Klett: Steph beneath the great sandstone arch, near Monticello, Utah 1982

BIOGRAPHIES

Robert Adams

American, born in Orange, New Jersey 1937
Studied English Literature at University of Redlands, California, 1955–59; PhD in English Literature at University of Southern California 1965. Lecturer and Assistant Professor of English, Colorado College, Colorado Springs, 1962–70. Independent photographer and writer since 1967. Widely exhibited since mid-1970s. Books include: THE NEW WEST: LANDSCAPES ALONG THE COLORADO FRONT RANGE, with an introduction by John Szarkowski, Boulder, Colorado 1974; DENVER: A PHOTOGRAPHIC SURVEY OF THE METROPOLITAN AREA, Boulder, Colorado 1977; PRAIRIE, Denver 1978; FROM THE MISSOURI WEST, Millerton, NY 1980; OUR LIVES AND OUR CHILDREN: PICTURES TAKEN NEAR THE ROCKY FLATS NUCLEAR WEAPONS PLANT, Millerton, NY 1984; and (forthcoming) ROBERT ADAMS: PHOTOGRAPHS 1965-85, Philadelphia Museum of Art and Aperture, NY. Writings were collected in BEAUTY IN PHOTOGRAPHY: ESSAYS IN DEFENSE OF TRADITIONAL VALUES, Millerton, NY 1981.

Dieter Appelt

German, born in Niemegk 1935
Studied at the Musikhochschule in Leipzig and Berlin, then photography - including experimental photography, under Professor Heinz Hajek-Halke at the Hochschule für Bildende Kunst, Berlin. Since 1982 Dieter Appelt has been a professor at the Hochschule der Künste, Berlin. A book on Dieter Appelt's work to date is forthcoming from Verlag Dirk Nishen, Berlin, in 1989.

Richard Avedon

American, born New York City 1923
Educated at De Witt Clinton High School and Columbia University. New York City's High School Poet Laureate, 1940. US Merchant Marines, 1942–44. Studied with Alexey Brodovitch at The Design Laboratory, New School of Social Research, 1944–50. Staff photographer for HARPER'S BAZAAR, 1945– 65. Editors: Carmel Snow, Diana Vreeland, Nancy White. Art Directors: Alexey Brodovitch, Henry Wolf, Marvin Israel, Ruth Ansel, Bea Feitler. Photographed the French Collections in Paris for HARPER'S BAZAAR and VOGUE, beginning 1947. Staff photographer for VOGUE from 1966. Editors: Alexander Liberman, Diana Vreeland, Grace Mirabella, Polly Mellen. Many awards for photography and commercial film direction. Major books: NOTHING PERSONAL, text by James Baldwin (1964); PORTRAITS, text by Harold Rosenberg (1976); AVEDON: PHOTOGRAPHS 1947-1977, text by

Harold Brodkey (1978). Major exhibitions: RICHARD AVEDON, Minneapolis Institute of Arts (1970); JACOB ISRAEL AVEDON, The Museum of Modern Art, New York (1974); AVEDON: PHOTOGRAPHS 1947-1977, The Metropolitan Museum of Art, New York. The plain but heroic style of the final portraits in this exhibition led on directly to the commission to photograph IN THE AMERICAN WEST. Opposing views on the Western portraits are: Dore Ashton, 'This Silent Theatre', ARTS, September 1985, pp. 136–144, and Max Kozloff, 'Through Eastern Eyes', ART IN AMERICA, January 1987, pp. 91–97.

Marvin Israel (1924–84) was well described by Owen Edwards, 'Marvin Israel, the Mentor', THE VILLAGE VOICE, 27 October 1975. His obituary appeared in THE NEW YORK TIMES, 8 May 1984.

John Baldessari

American, born National City, California 1931
Studied painting at San Diego State College, California, 1949–53. Taught in colleges in San Diego, 1953–70. Professor, California Institute of Arts, Los Angeles, since 1970. Widely exhibited in USA and Europe since 1970; regular shows at his gallery, Sonnabend, New York City. Participated in 'The Extended Document' exhibition, George Eastman House, 1975. His films were shown at Artists' Space and the Whitney Museum of American Art, New York, 1978. As teacher and artist he is of vital importance to, for example, Richard Prince and his generation of artists. His place in this development is indicated in Andy Grundberg and Kathleen McCarthy Gauss's PHOTOGRAPHY AND ART, INTERACTIONS SINCE 1946 (New York, 1987). An important catalogue is JOHN BALDESSARI, with essays by Marcia Tucker and Robert Pincus-Witten, The New Museum, New York, 1981. See also the interview article 'No More Boring Art' by Hunter Drohojowska in ARTnews, January 1986, pp. 62–69. A fuller bibliography appears in CONTEMPORARY PHOTOGRAPHERS, ed. Colin Naylor et al, Chicago and London 1988.

Lewis Baltz

American, born Newport Beach, California, 1945
Educated at the San Francisco Art Institute, 1967–69 and Claremont Graduate School, California, 1969–71. Freelance photographer in California since 1970. Exhibited at Castelli Graphics, New York, in 1971 and regularly since then – also internationally. His publications include THE NEW INDUSTRIAL PARKS NEAR IRVINE, CALIFORNIA (New York, 1975); MARYLAND, edited by Jane Livingston, Washington D. C. 1976; NEVADA, New York 1978; PARK CITY, with text by Gus Blaisdell, New York 1980; SAN QUENTIN POINT, with essay by

Mark Haworth-Booth, New York and West Berlin 1986; edited CONTEMPORARY AMERICAN PHOTOGRAPHIC WORKS, with introduction by John Upton, Houston, 1977. See also 'Konsumterror: Notes on Late Industrial Alienation', APERTURE, New York, Fall 1984. CANDLESTICK PARK, a new series of works, was shown at Galerie Michèle Chomette, Paris, November 1988. Lewis Baltz is currently resident in Milan.

Nancy Burson

American, born St. Louis, Missouri, 1948
Studied painting at Colorado Women's College in Denver. Moved to New York City, 1968. Saw the exhibition 'The Machine as Seen at the End of the Industrial Age', The Museum of Modern Art, and conceived the idea of making an 'age machine', a video screen where you could see yourself change in front of your own eyes. She took this idea to EAT, Robert Rauschenberg's Experiments in Art and Technology, an organisation linking artists and scientists. She learned that technology was not available to realize her ideas. She exhibited her paintings at Bertha Urdang Gallery (1974) and Hal Bromm Gallery (1977) in New York City. She continued to seek ways of imaging aging and in the late 1970s worked with the MIT engineer Tom Schneider, who eventually designed the basic interpolation that allowed Burson to alter and change faces. They share a patent – The Method and Apparatus for Producing an Image of a Person's Face at a Different Age. She met Carling and Kramlich in 1980. Their work has been widely exhibited, published and televised, and is described by William A. Ewing and Jeanne A. McDermott in the book COMPOSITES, COMPUTER-GENERATED PORTRAITS, BY NANCY BURSON, RICHARD CARLING AND DAVID KRAMLICH, New York 1986. Nancy Burson has more recently made a series of works which mix works by painters.

Helen Chadwick

British, born Croydon 1953
Studied at Brighton Polytechnic 1973–76, Chelsea School of Art 1976–77. First solo exhibition 'Model Institutions', Newcastle Polytechnic and tour 1981–84. Group exhibitions include 'Aperto 84', Venice Biennale. Widely exhibited in 1980s. OF MUTABILITY, published by the Institute of Contemporary Arts, London (1986) contains 'In the Garden of Delights,' by Marina Warner and 'Contesting Alienation' by Richard Cork. OF MUTABILITY is also an ICA video: 'Helen Chadwick in conversation with Marina Warner' (1986) and there is a film titled OF MUTABILITY, directed by Chris Rawlence, ICA TV, for Channel 4 (1987). A book on Helen Chadwick's work to date is forthcoming from Secker & Warburg, London, in 1989.

Martin Cleaver

British, born in Handsworth, Birmingham, 1956
Educated at West Bromwich College of Commerce and Technology, Wednesbury. Joined the Press Association, London 1974. Photographed the Iranian Embassy siege, 1979. Chosen as one of two photographers to cover the British Task Force on its way to the South Atlantic and the subsequent hostilities with Argentina. Was in the South Atlantic for three months, including one month on land. Cleaver was based on the aircraft carrier HMS HERMES and was to cover the navy task force spearhead with HMS BROADSWORD, HMS INVINCIBLE and other ships, using the darkrooms and other facilities on the Royal Fleet Auxiliary supply ships. Martin Cleaver joined the Associated Press, in London, in 1987.

Kate Salway's article 'Over in a Flash' appeared in PHOTO-GRAPHY, London, in June 1987.

Lynne Cohen

Canadian, born Racine, Wisconsin, USA 1944
Educated University College London and University of Wisconsin. Artist and photographer based in Ottawa since 1973. Now teaches at University of Ottawa. She has used an 8 x 10 inch (203 x 253 mm) view camera since 1972. She began the interiors series 20 years ago. Her work has been widely exhibited and collected by The Art Institute of Chicago, the International Museum of Photography at George Eastman House, Rochester, NY, and other museums.

Lee Friedlander

American, born Aberdeen, Washington, 1934
Studied photography at Art Center School, Los Angeles, under Edward Kaminski, 1953–55. Began photographing at age 14. Freelance since 1955: ESQUIRE, McCALL'S, COLLIER'S, ART IN AMERICA, jazz record covers, etc. First solo exhibition at International Museum of Photography, George Eastman House, Rochester, NY 1963. Subsequently exhibited world-wide. Among his many important publications are WORK FROM THE SAME HOUSE, with Jim Dine, London and New York 1969; SELF-PORTRAIT, New City, New York 1970; THE AMERICAN MONUMENT, text by Leslie George Katz, New York 1976; LEE FRIEDLANDER: PHOTOGRAPHS, New City, New York 1978; FLOWERS AND TREES, New York, 1981; FACTORY VALLEYS: OHIO AND PENNSYLVANIA, New York 1982; CRAY AT CHIPPEWA FALLS, Minneapolis, Minnesota 1987; LEE FRIEDLANDER, a Photo

Poche, was published by the Centre National de la Photographie, Paris 1987. Friedlander and his associates have set very high standards for design and production. FACTORY VALLEYS, published by Callaway Editions, was printed in 300-line screen duotone offset lithography by the Meriden Gravure Company from negatives by Richard Benson. The book was designed by Nicholas Callaway and Anne Kennedy. CRAY AT CHIPPEWA FALLS was published by Cray Research, Inc., and printed in 300-line screen tritone offset lithography by Franklin Graphics, Inc., from negatives by Richard Benson.

Masahisa Fukase

Japanese, born in Bifuka, Hokkaido 1934
Studied photography at the Nihon University, Tokyo. Worked as a photographer for the Daiichi Advertising Company, Tokyo, 1956–65, and for the Nihon Design Centre and Kawada Shobo, 1965–68. Freelance photographer since 1968. His solo exhibitions include: SKY OVER AN OIL REFINERY, Konishiroku Gallery, Tokyo 1960; A SLAUGHTERHOUSE, Ginza Gallery, Tokyo 1961; BIG FIGHT, Waren House, Seibu, Tokyo 1973; AHA!/CROWS, Ginza Nikon Salon, Tokyo; YOHKO, Nikon Salon, Tokyo. He appeared in NEW JAPANESE PHOTOGRAPHY, The Museum of Modern Art, New York, 1974 (and US tour) and in other important international exhibitions of work from Japan, including BLACK SUN: THE EYES OF FOUR (Eikoh Hosoe, Shomei Tomatsu, Masahisa Fukase and Daido Moriyama), The Museum of Modern Art, Oxford, the Serpentine Gallery, London, The Philadelphia Museum of Art, the catalogue by Mark Holborn published as APERTURE No.102, Spring 1986, and in book form. Mark Holborn has also written on Fukase in CONTEMPORARY PHOTOGRAPHERS, ed. C. Naylor et al., Chicago and London 1988 (2nd ed.). Fukase's books include HOMO LUDENS (Tokyo 1971) and YOHKO (1978). RAVENS was published, with an introduction by Akira Hasegawa, by Sokyu-sha, Yokohama, Japan in 1986.

Frank Gohlke

American, born Wichita Falls, Texas 1942
Educated at the University of Texas, 1960–64; BA in English literature, 1964; Yale University, 1964–67; MA in English literature 1967. Studied photography with Paul Caponigro, 1967–68. Freelance photographer since 1967. Has also taught, including Visiting Professorship at Yale University Graduate School, 1981. Selected group exhibitions include 'New Topographics: Photographs of a Man-Altered Landscape', International Museum of Topography, George Eastman House, Rochester, NY 1975, and 'Mirrors and Windows:

American Photography since 1960', The Museum of Modern Art, New York 1978 and tour. Frank Gohlke's LANDSCAPES FROM THE MIDDLE OF THE WORLD appeared in 1988 as an exhibition and publication issued by The Friends of Photography, San Francisco, and The Museum of Contemporary Photography, Chicago. The publication is published as UNTITLED 46 by The Friends of Photography and is introduced by Ben Lifson. Gohlke's photographs from Mount St. Helens are to be published in book form by Johns Hopkins University Press. He has also executed a photomural commission for Tulsa Oklahoma Airport in 1980 (described by Rob Silberman in ART IN AMERICA, July 1985). Gohlke has described his Mt. St. Helens project in 'A Volatile Core', APERTURE No.98, Spring 1985.

John R. Gossage

American, born in New York City 1946
Studied privately with Lisette Model, Alexey Brodovitch and Bruce Davidson, New York City 1962–64. Freelance photographer, New York, 1963–64 and in Washington, DC since 1965. Exhibited widely since mid-1970s. Books: GARDENS, with text by Walter Hopps, New York and Washington, DC 1978; AMERICAN IMAGES, New York 1979; THE POND, Millerton, NY 1985; STADT DES SCHWARZ, Washington, DC 1987; LAMF – THREE DAYS IN BERLIN, Washington, DC 1988.

Megan Jenkinson

New Zealand, born Hamilton, NZ, 1958
Educated at Elam School of Fine Arts, University of Auckland, 1976–79. Awarded Bachelor of Arts in Photography, 1980. Colour photography technician, Real Pictures, Auckland, 1981–83. Teaching colour photography and other aspects of photography, plus travel to USA, Europe, Japan, 1984–85. Full-time lecturer in Photography at Elam School of Fine Arts, University of Auckland, since 1985. She has exhibited regularly in New Zealand and also with the Polaroid Collection (Photokina, Cologne, 1984, 1988 and travelling) and showed her work in a solo exhibition at The Photographers' Gallery, London in 1985. Her work was also shown in 'NZXI', Auckland City Art Gallery 1988 (exhibition catalogue published).

Astrid Klein

German, born Cologne 1951
Studied at the Fachhochschule für Kunst und Design, Cologne, 1973–77, working in gouache on black canvases. She began to make large-scale photoworks incorporating news and magazine photographs in 1978. Her first solo exhibition was held at the Hamburger Künstlerhaus in 1980. She has subsequently shown widely in Europe and more recently in the United States, and in the biennales in Sydney and Venice. She is represented by Produzentengalerie, Hamburg. Her work was included in 'Reste des Authentischen' (Museum Folkwang, Essen), which travelled in Britain in 1987–88 and in the Tate Gallery's 'Art from Europe' (1987), with an exhibition of her new work appearing at the Institute of Contemporary Arts, London, in January 1989.

Robert Mapplethorpe

American, born New York City 1946
Educated at Pratt Institute, Brooklyn, New York, 1963–70. Underground film-maker, New York, 1965–70. Photographer, collagist, assemblagist, New York, 1970–72. Independent photographer since 1972. Early work with appropriated photographs, Polaroids, coloured surfaces and customised frames. Exhibitions held regularly since 1976. Also appeared in 'The Collection of Sam Wagstaff' (Corcoran Gallery, Washington, DC, the Grey Art Gallery, New York University, 1977–78) and 'Mirrors and Windows: American Photography since 1960' (The Museum of Modern Art, New York, 1978 and subsequent tour). A full bibliography is given in Richard Marshall's ROBERT MAPPLETHORPE, with essays by Richard Howard and Ingrid Sischy, published by the Whitney Museum of American Art, New York, in association with New York Graphic Society Books and Little, Brown and Company, Boston, 1988 (English edition, Secker & Warburg).

Nicholas Nixon

American, born Detroit, Michigan 1947
Studied American literature at the University of Michigan, Ann Arbor, 1965–69; studied art at the University of New Mexico, 1973–74. Married Bebe Brown in 1971. Worked as an independent photographer, based in Cambridge, Massachusetts, since 1974. Exhibited in 'New Topographics: Photographs of a Man-Altered Landscape', International Museum of Photography, George Eastman House, Rochester, NY, 1975. Solo exhibition at The Museum of Modern Art, New York, 1976. Has exhibited widely since. His subjects include architecture, people, age, family life and – most recently and continuing, victims of AIDS. He showed series on seven different sufferers from the disease in October 1988 at Zabriskie Gallery, New York. One series, devoted to Tom Moran, August 1987 to February 1988, is illustrated in his exhibition catalogue NICHOLAS NIXON: PICTURES OF PEOPLE, introduced by Peter Galassi, published by The Museum of Modern Art, New York (1988) which also contains a bibliography.

Paul de Nooijer

Dutch, born Eindhoven 1943
Studied industrial design at the Akademie voor Industriele Vormgeving, Eindhoven 1960–63. Freelance advertising/illustration photographer, Eindhoven 1968–73. Freelance photographer and film-maker since 1974. Has exhibited widely since the early 1970s, received major awards and commissions for murals. Publications include: LOSING ONE'S HEAD, introduction by Ingeborg Th. Leijerzapf, Eindhoven 1978; LOSING ONE'S PHOTOS, Eindhoven 1981; SQUARES, text by Hripsimé Visser, Middelburg 1987.

Richard Prince

American, born Panama Canal Zone, 1949
Brought up in New England, began drawing in childhood but did not attend an art school. He did, however, train with artists in Boston and Paris, where he studied painting, printmaking, sculpture and art history. Began to photograph advertising images in 1977, cropping text out of the picture and arranging similar subjects in sets. This work first shown at the Karl Ernst Jollenbeck Galerie, Cologne. First solo exhibition at Artists' Space, New York. One-man show at Metro Pictures, New York 1981 and again in 1982 when he showed 'Sunsets': each work was composed of a black and white cutout advertising image, set in front of a colour sunburst background and photographed. Began 'Entertainers' series, 1982; first exhibited 'Cowboys' 1983; published a novel, WHY I GO TO THE MOVIES ALONE (Tanam Press, New York) 1983. Produced first of 'Gangs' series – groups of related images reproduced in a grid formation – in 1984, including 'Girlfriends' taken from biker magazines. More recent work crops imagery from pornography and Vietnam battle scenes and his work in 1986–88 simultaneously tells, transforms and dissects jokes. His work has been discussed as part of Postmodernism, alongside the imagery of Cindy Sherman, Barbara Kruger, Sherrie Levine and others concerned with mass-produced imagery, simulation and 'hyperreality'. Interviews appear in APERTURE, No.100 (with David Robbins), 1985; with Jeffrey Rian in ART IN AMERICA, March 1987. See also Kate Linker 'On Richard Prince's Photographs', ARTS MAGAZINE, November 1982, and the books PHOTOGRAPHY AND ART: INTERACTIONS SINCE 1946 by Andy Grundberg and Kathleen McCarthy Gauss (New York, 1987) and THIS IS NOT A PHOTOGRAPH: TWENTY YEARS OF LARGE-SCALE PHOTOGRAPHY, 1966–86, Sarasota, Fla.1987. RICHARD PRINCE, exhibition catalogue, text by Jeffrey Rian, published by Centre National d'Art Contemporain de Grenoble, France 1988.

Sebastião Salgado

Brazilian, born 1944
Salgado was trained as an economist, employed by the International Coffee Organization. After a number of trips to Africa for this organization he decided to become a photographer, beginning his career at the age of 29. His first reportage was on famine in Niger. He photographed the condition of migrant workers in Europe. He has worked for a wide variety of magazines, newspapers and humanitarian organizations. He reported on the return of democracy in Portugal, the independence of Angola and the devastation brought by famine to Africa. His extensive documentation of the latter, made in conjunction with the French relief group 'Médecins sans Frontières', was published in France in 1986 as the book SAHEL: L'HOMME EN DÉTRESSE (SAHEL: MAN IN DISTRESS). Salgado is a member of the photographic agency Magnum Photos and lives in Paris but returns frequently to photograph in Latin America. He received the W. Eugene Smith Award for Humanistic Photography in 1983. His book OTHER AMERICAS was published by Pantheon Books, New York, in 1986.

Michael Schmidt

German, born Berlin 1945
Self taught in photography. Freelance since 1965. Instructor in photography at Volkshochschule, Berlin-Kreuzberg, since 1969. Also taught at Universität FB 4, Essen, 1979–80. Has exhibited widely since the late 1970s. His publications include BERLIN-KREUZBERG, West Berlin 1973; BERLIN: STADTLANDSCHAFT UND MENSCHEN, with text by Heinz Ohff, West Berlin 1978; BERLIN-WEDDING, with text by Heinz Ohff, West Berlin 1978; MICHAEL SCHMIDT: STADTLANDSCHAFTEN, Essen, West Germany 1981; MICHAEL SCHMIDT: BERLIN-KREUZBERG STADTBILDER, West Berlin 1983; MICHAEL SCHMIDT: BILDER 1979–1986, Spectrum/Sprengel Museum, Hannover 1987. WAFFENRUHE was shown at the Berlinische Galerie in 1987

and at the Museum Folkwang, Essen in 1988. Michael Schmidt showed in 'New Work 4' at The Museum of Modern Art, New York in 1988.

Cindy Sherman

American, born Glen Ridge, New Jersey 1954
Educated at State University College, Buffalo, New York (BA, 1976). Resides in New York City. First solo exhibition, Hallwalls, Buffalo, NY, 1979. Solo exhibitions in 1980 at Contemporary Arts Museum, Houston, The Kitchen, New York, and Metro Pictures, New York. Regular exhibitions at Metro Pictures, her agents, since 1980, and widely in United States and around the world. Her earliest series of Untitled Film Stills established her reputation. Her work has been summarized as 'deconstructing the image of the white girl as eternal fantasy object' (by Margo Jefferson in a thought-provoking recent article, 'The Image Culture: Michael Jackson, Cindy Sherman, and the art of self-manipulation', in VOGUE, NY, March 1988). After the fashion series Sherman worked with the imagery of fairy tales, nightmares, dismemberment and decomposition. Her work has appeared in many major exhibitions and publications as well as the Channel Four TV series 'State of the Art' (1986). Her retrospective exhibition catalogue published by The Whitney Musem of American Art, New York, contains essays by Peter Schjeldahl and Lisa Phillips (1987).

Doug and Mike Starn

American, born New Jersey 1961
Identical twins, brought up in southern New Jersey and educated at the School of the Museum of Fine Arts, Boston. They have received grants from the National Endowment for the Arts, the Massachusetts Council on the Arts, and the School of the Museum of Fine Arts, Boston. Began exhibiting 1984. First 'solo' exhibition, Stux Gallery, Boston, 1985 (then annually in the Stux Gallery spaces either in Boston or New York). Included in the Whitney Biennial 1987. A bibliography is provided in DOUG AND MIKE STARN, THE CHRIST SERIES (Projects 1, The John and Mable Ringing Museum of Art, Sarasota, Fla., 1987). See also THE STARN TWINS: THE HORSES (ICA EDITION), Stux Gallery, New York, 1987. Also exhibited in 'N.Y. Art Now, The Saatchi Collection Part II', 1988. A useful article is Gary Indiana, 'Imitation of Life', THE VILLAGE VOICE, 29 April 1986.

Hiromi Tsuchida

Japanese, born Fukui Prefecture, 1939
Graduated from the Faculty of Engineering, Fukui University, 1963. Joined Pola Cosmetics, Inc. as researcher. Graduated from the Tokyo College of Photography, 1966. Left Pola Cosmetics in 1971 to become a freelance photographer. His work was included in NEW JAPANESE PHOTOGRAPHY at The Museum of Modern Art, New York, in 1974 and in group exhibitions held in Vienna, Amsterdam and Bologna. He was also represented in SELF-PORTRAIT JAPAN at the International Center of Photography, New York, 1979. In 1976 he published ZOKU-SHIN: GODS OF THE EARTH, an abrasive study of the realities of modern Japanese life centred on festivals and religious ceremonies photographed by Tsuchida in rural areas. His work has been widely exhibited and published in Japan, where he has also received major awards. 'Hiroshima' was exhibited at the Visual Studies Workshop, Rochester, New York, in 1985.

Woody Vasulka

Born Brno, Czechoslovakia in 1937, lives United States
Studied metal technologies and hydraulic mechanics at the School of Industrial Engineering, Brno. Then entered the Academy of Performing Arts, Faculty of Film and Television, Prague, where he began to direct and produce short films. He emigrated to the United States in 1965 and freelanced in New York City as a film editor for the next years. In 1967 he began experiments with electronic sounds, stroboscopic lights and (two years later) with video. In 1974 he became a faculty member of the Center for Media Study at State University in New York, Buffalo and began his investigations into computer controlled video. He constructed 'The Image Articulator', a real time digital video tool. With his wife Steina, he founded 'The Kitchen', an important interdisciplinary art centre in New York. He has participated in many major video shows in the States and abroad, lectured, published articles, composed music and made numerous video tapes. Guggenheim Fellowship, 1979. Made THE COMMISSION (an electronic opera) in 1984. The Vasulkas are now preparing a major retrospective of their work at The American Museum of the Moving Image, New York. A catalogue of works by Steina and Woody Vasulka was published by the Albright-Knox Art Gallery, Buffalo, New York, in 1978. Introduction by Linda Cathcart. Anne H. Hoy provided valuable programme notes for the showing of the then unfinished ART OF MEMORY at the International Center of Photography, New York, in September–October 1987.

Bruce Weber

American, born in Greensburg, Pennsylvania 1946
Education included Denison University, Ohio; New York University Art and Film School; New School for Social Research, New York City. Exhibited widely since the early 1980s. ATHLETES, the subject of his first book (titled BRUCE WEBER, Los Angeles 1984), was exhibited in San Francisco, London, Paris and New York, where it was presented by his gallery, Robert Miller Gallery. He has exhibited there regularly since, including O RIO DE JANEIRO (his second book, published in New York in 1986). A multi-frame work called 'Studio Wall' was exhibited at the Whitney Museum of American Art 1987 Biennial exhibition. He has won many awards for his work as photographer and film-maker and in video. His films (Director/Producer) are BROKEN NOSES (1987) and LET'S GET LOST (1988). Martin Harrison discusses Bruce Weber in SHOTS OF STYLE: GREAT FASHION PHOTOGRAPHS CHOSEN BY DAVID BAILEY (Victoria and Albert Museum, London 1985) and an informative article by Michael Gross, 'Bruce Weber, Camera Chameleon', appeared in VANITY FAIR, New York, in June 1986. See also John Gossage on Weber in the exhibition catalogue FUTURE OF PHOTOGRAPHY, Corcoran Art Gallery, Washington, DC, 1987.

William Wegman

American, born Holyoke, Massachusetts 1943
Trained as a painter at Massachusetts College of Art, Boston and at University of Illinois, Urbana. First solo exhibition at Sonnabend Gallery, Paris 1971. Has exhibited widely and often in Europe and USA. Also a video artist. His photographic collaboration with 'Man Ray' was published as MAN'S BEST FRIEND (New York, 1983). Has regularly used the Polaroid 20 x 24 camera since the Polaroid Corporation first invited him to use it in 1978. His video DOG BASEBALL, featuring Fay Ray as Pitcher, was screened on SATURDAY NIGHT LIVE in 1987. Wegman continues to work as a painter as well as portrait photographer and recently designed 'La Jolla Vista View', which resembles a landscaped scenic overlook: 'Behind a low wall commanding a broad panorama of the surrounding area will be mounted a telescope through which to study the local landmarks. But what that telescope will scan are the encroaching signs of suburban sprawl, a constantly developing landscape of increasingly densely packed condominiums, freeways, and shopping centers'. A 12 foot long bronze plaque on the wall will carry Wegman's drawn commentary on the scene (ARTFORUM, April 1988, p. 128). Wegman is well described by Amy Hempel in 'The Artist and his Dog', THE NEW YORK TIMES MAGAZINE, 29 November, 1987.

ACKNOWLEDGEMENTS

We wish to express our warm thanks to all of the authors whose writings we have quoted in this book, and in particular Aperture, a division of Silver Mountain Foundation, Inc., New York, and the author, for permission to quote from David Byrne's introduction to OCCUPIED TERRITORY by Lynne Cohen, published by Aperture (1987); the Institute of Contemporary Arts, London, and the author for permission to quote from Marina Warner's essay 'In the Garden of Delight' in Helen Chadwick's catalogue OF MUTABILITY published by the Institute of Contemporary Arts in 1986; David Lodge and Secker and Warburg Ltd for an extract from David Lodge's novel NICE WORK published by Secker and Warburg Ltd in 1988; Lewis Baltz and the editors of CAMERA AUSTRIA, Graz, for permission to quote from his essay on WAFFENRUHE by Michael Schmidt.

Many individuals and institutions have generously provided information, help and advice during the preparation of PHOTOGRAPHY NOW and we wish to thank them all, in particular Shelley Dowell at Richard Avedon, Inc., New York; David Travis, Curator of Photography, The Art Institute of Chicago; Philip Miller, Agfa-Gevaert Ltd., London; Ben Stocks, Collett, Dickenson, Pearce & Partners, London; Peter Turner, CREATIVE CAMERA, London; Ute Eskildsen, Curator, Fotografische Sammlung, Museum Folkwang, Essen; Christine Frisinghelli and Manfred Willman, Forum Stadtpark, Graz; Els Barents, Curator of Photography, Stedelijk Museum, Amsterdam; Bas Vroege, Director, Perspektief Gallery, Rotterdam; Michèle Chomette, Paris; Nathan Lyons, Director, The Visual Studies Workshop, Rochester, New York; Sue Davies, The Photographers' Gallery, London; Michel Frizot, Centre National de la Photographie, Paris; Kathleen McCarthy Gauss, Curator of Photography, The Los Angeles County Museum of Art; David Goldblatt, Johannesburg; Anna Harding, Director, Camerawork, London; Michael E. Hoffman, Publisher, Aperture, New York; Professor Eikoh Hosoe, Tokyo; Martin Harrison, Northampton; Marvin Heiferman, New York; Willis Hartshhorn, International Center of Photography, New York; Mark Holborn, London; Maureen O. Paley, Director, Interim Art, London; Sylviane de Decker Heftler, Paris; Chris Killip, Newcastle-on-Tyne; Wilmar Koenig, Berlin; Peter MacGill, Pace/MacGill Gallery, New York; Josef Koudelka, Paris; James Lingwood, Institute of Contemporary Arts, London; Jeffrey Fraenkel Gallery, San Francisco; Robert Mann, New York; Denise Miller-Clark, Director, The Museum of Contemporary Photography, Columbia College, Chicago; Harry H. Lunn, Paris; John Szarkowski, Director, and Peter Galassi and Susan Kismaric, Associate Curators, Department of Photography, The Museum of Modern Art, New York; Maria Morris Hambourg, Curator of Photographs, The Metropolitan Museum of Art, New York; Alain Seyag, Curator of Photographs, Musée National d'Art Moderne, Centre Georges Pompidou, Paris; Howard Read III, Robert Miller Gallery, New York; Carol T. Hartwell, Curator of Photographs, The Minneapolis Institute of Arts; Barbara Gladstone and Sophie Hager Hume, Barbara Gladstone Gallery, New York; Stefan Stux and Anne R. Pasternak, Stux Gallery, New York; Janelle Reiring and colleagues at Metro Pictures, New York; François Hebel, Director, and Agnès Sire, Magnum Photos, Paris; Neil Burgess, Magnum Photos, London; Daniela Mrazkova, Prague; Pedro Meyer, Mexico City; Trisha Ziff, Network Photographers, London; Jeffrey Gilbert, formerly Curator of Photographs at the Museum of Modern Art, Kyoto; Kotaro Iizawa, Tokyo; Eelco Wolf, Director of Communications, and Barbara Hitchcock, Curator of the collection, Polaroid Corporation, Boston; Jan Hnizdo, Polaroid GmbH, Offenbach; Belinda Mobbs, Polaroid (UK) Ltd.; Fred Ritchin, Brooklyn; Sam Roubini, DS Colour International Ltd., London; Fred Baldwin and Wendy Watriss,

Houston; Renee van der Vloodt, London; Virginia Zabriskie, Ann LaPides and Loic Malle, Zabriskie Gallery, New York and Paris.

I should also like to thank the many colleagues at the Victoria & Albert Museum who have unsparingly helped in every way, particularly John Murdoch, Keeper of the Department of Designs, Prints and Drawings, Chris Titterington, Assistant Curator of Photographs, and Lesley Burton, Publications Officer. Finally, it has been a great pleasure to work with Dirk Nishen and his team on every aspect of this book.

Mark Haworth-Booth